Art of South Indian Cooking

Art of South Indian Cooking

Alamelu Vairavan
and
Patricia Marquardt

HIPPOCRENE BOOKS
New York

For information, address:
HIPPOCRENE BOOKS, INC.
171 Madison Avenue
New York, NY 10016

Library of Congress Cataloging-in-Publication Data
Vairavan, Alamelu.
Art of south Indian cooking / Alamelu Vairavan and Patricia Marquardt.
p.   cm.
Includes index.
ISBN 0-7818-0525-2
1. Cookery, India.   I. Marquardt, Patricia.   II. Title.
TX724.V33   1997

641.5954'8—dc21   97 to   24996
                                                         CIP

Printed in the United States of America.

DEDICATION

This book is dedicated to the cherished memory of
Aiyah RM. Kasiviswanathan Chettiar,
Ayal Valliammai Achi
and
William Marquardt
for their love and inspiration.

CONTENTS

Acknowledgments

Alamelu would like to express her deep appreciation to her husband Dr. K. Vairavan, both for encouraging the writing of this cookbook and for his loving guidance throughout the lengthy project.

The authors would also like to thank the following people for their generous support and inspiration:

Valli Vairavan
Ashok Kasi Vairavan
Dr. A. Alagappan
Visalakshi Alagappan
Chettinad Chef Natesan
Maya Sikdar
Sree Devi Vinnakota
Dr. Prakash Ambegaonkar
Nandini Ambegaonkar
Dr. Pradeep Rohatgi
Dr. Kalpana Rohatgi
PL. Lakshmi
AV.M. Palaniappan
Umayal Palaniappan
Dr. Ichiro Suzuki

The authors are also grateful to the numerous other people who have given us helpful suggestions throughout the writing of this book, especially to   Ms. Carol Chitnis, Cookbook Editor of Hippocrene Books. Special thanks to the many wonderful people who provided hospitality and guidance during the authors' research trip to South India in early 1996.

PREFACE
by Alamelu Vairavan

I was born and raised in Madras, South India. I grew up in a large household with a professional cook and regularly shared in an abundance of delicious foods. Although I knew nothing about cooking itself, I did greatly enjoy good food. After my marriage in 1967, I accompanied my husband to the U.S. as a young bride. Necessity, as they say, is the mother of invention. I learned cooking in New York from a professional cook at my aunt's house under a most disciplined but enjoyable regime, imposed by my aunt Visa Alagappan, while my husband was finishing his Ph.D. thesis at the University of Notre Dame. Following my cooking lessons and orientation to American life in New York, I joined my husband at Notre Dame.

To my surprise, I found immediate joy in cooking. I am a person who loves the company of people and who loves to entertain. In the past twenty-seven years, my husband and I have entertained numerous friends and family from all over the world. Whenever friends dined with us, they indicated how much they enjoyed the food. Many even asked me for the recipes. These compliments not only gave me joy but have inspired me greatly. I have also given numerous cooking demonstrations in the community, participated in block party contributions for neighbors and friends, and conducted local cooking classes. All these activities encouraged my interest in cooking very much. As my interest grew, I discovered that there is hardly any book on South Indian cooking written in English. This fact, in addition to repeated requests for recipes and my own growing interest in cooking, convinced me to write a South Indian cookbook. Another motivating factor has been my desire to pass on my recipes to our children and to the generations to come. For all those who so often requested such a cookbook, here it is: *The Art of South Indian Cooking*.

My co-author, my dearest friend and neighbor, Dr. Patricia Marquardt, is a born cook. Pat enjoys cooking and loves to explore different cuisines. Whenever Pat tried one of my Indian dishes for the first time, she would come to me with great enthusiasm and say, "This food is divine. How did you make it?" Pat also enjoys using various herbs and spices to flavor food and is particularly fond of vegetarian dishes. After Pat learned a few Indian dishes, she encouraged me to sample her cooking, which I also found to be marvelous. My very dear husband, Dr. K. Vairavan (K.V.), realized how much I enjoyed cooking and suggested that I ask Pat to be the co-author of an Indian cookbook. When I asked Pat, she was delighted, and together we set out on the exciting adventure of writing this book. I was thrilled to have Pat observe my cooking, ask questions, request precise measurements of the ingredients, and help write the recipes in an organized manner. K.V., Bill (Pat's late husband), and our children Valli and Ashok provided the ongoing inspiration which kept the project alive despite many lengthy interruptions. Our collaboration, which began several years ago with a vision of a good South Indian cookbook accessible to today's cooks, now culminates in this publication.

This cookbook is very different from other Indian cookbooks on the market. The majority of these books describe North Indian cooking and emphasize an abundance of meat dishes. This cookbook specializes in South Indian cooking. In South India, people have learned to cook with various vegetables and spices to add flavor to the food. Rice is a staple food in South India and can be cooked in many different ways. It is traditionally served with a variety of vegetables cooked with different dals (lentils) and spices. The many kinds of dals commonly used in South Indian cooking are a great source of protein. As more and more Americans are discovering, vegetarian meals can be diverse and delicious. Eating rice with a variety of vegetables cooked in different dals and spices can be a healthy, satisfying experience. In South India, meat is used only as a side dish. Since I grew up in a non-vegetarian family, however, you will also find recipes using chicken, lamb, shrimp and fish in this book.

A typical South Indian breakfast may include crisp dosas (a kind of thin pancake made with rice and urad dal), white fluffy idlis (steamed rice cakes) and vadas (doughnut-shaped fritters made with lentils) served with sambhar and chutney. Other breakfast items such as pongal (creamy spiced or sweetened rice) and uppuma(cream of wheat or rice cooked with spices) are also served during night meals or for evening tea. For lunch, rice is served first with sambhar or kulambu, a thick stewlike sauce made of dals and vegetables, then with rasam, a thin, spicy soup, followed by plain yogurt to be mixed with rice. A variety of vegetables, such as kootu and poriyal and also pappadam, are served with all of the above three courses. Kootu is a vegetable cooked with dal, ginger, cumin and garlic, while poriyal is a drier stir-fried vegetable dish. Pappadam is a crispy wafer- like accompaniment made from urad dal and spices which enhances a meal. A South Indian dinner is usually a light meal and may consist of rice and vegetables, or idli or dosa served with sambhar or chutney.

Many Indian and American friends who had disliked certain vegetables (e.g. brussel sprouts, lima beans, broccoli) were surprised at how much they actually started liking these foods when prepared in the South Indian manner and began asking for more. You too may be surprised. I have tried this experiment on many who disliked certain vegetables with the same, happy result. The long list of spices called for by many Indian recipes may be discouraging to the novice cook. But spices, such as cumin, coriander, turmeric, fenugreek, black mustard seeds, fennel, and red peppers are easily available on the spice rack of most supermarkets and gourmet shops. Those that are not available there can be bought economically from Indian or specialty grocery stores. Also, once you assemble a basic pantry of Indian spices, you will be able to use them time and again in numerous recipes which often call for the same ingredients in similar order. I have used corn oil or pure vegetable oil in most of my recipes because of its mild flavor and healthfulness. Regular stainless steel heavy bottomed sauce pans, nonstick pots and pans and cast-iron skillets can be used in Indian cooking. Electric rice cookers and woks are useful but not necessary.

Electric blenders, however, are necessary.

Our book will encourage you to cook many unique, appealing, and tasty dishes. If you are looking for a healthy and delicious diet look to the cuisine of South India. In India, cooking is often considered an act of reverence and joy. When you take the culinary journey to South India, you too will be uplifted in body and spirit!

Alamelu Vairavan
September, 1997
Milwaukee, Wisconsin

About the Author

Alamelu Vairavan was born and raised in South India. Shortly after her marriage in 1967, she joined her husband at the University of Notre Dame, where he was a graduate student. She moved to Wisconsin in 1968 with her husband. She attended the University of Wisconsin-Milwaukee, while raising a family, and graduated with a B.S. degree in Health Information Management in the School of Allied Health.

Alamelu has worked for more than a decade in the Long Term Care (Nursing Home) health care field. She has also served as a Clinical Instructor for the University of Wisconsin-Milwaukee. In addition, she has served as a nursing home consultant in Health Information Management for various other health care facilities. Alamelu received her Wisconsin Nursing Home Administrator's license in May, 1992, and she is currently the supervisor of Health Information Management at the SevenOaks Long Term Care facility in Glendale, Wisconsin.

PREFACE
by Patricia Marquardt

Working with Alamelu on the writing of this cookbook has been a very pleasurable learning experience for me. Tantalized by the richly exotic aromas emanating from Alamelu's kitchen and by the tasty foods she sent next door for me to sample, I soon immersed myself in the exciting world of South Indian cooking. Beets vada and lemon rice were my first efforts at Indian cooking, but now, thanks to the knowledge gained from closely observing Alamelu at work in her kitchen over many months, my repertoire of Indian dishes has broadened considerably.

Without a doubt, Alamelu is an experienced and uniquely gifted cook (as her many guests attest), but her recipes are clearly set forth and are not difficult for even a novice cook to follow. The wide variety of ingredients used in the recipes gives an incomparably rich flavor to the dishes, even to simple vegetables such as spinach and brussels sprouts (which now appear regularly on the table at our house). Although the number of Indian seasonings and spices used in the recipes may, at first glance, appear to be overwhelming, the cook will soon learn that similar, if not identical, spice mixtures are used in many other recipes. It is even possible to make mixtures of the spices ahead of time and keep them on hand for ready use in preparing the various recipes. Nor is it necessary to make the dishes too spicy. This aspect of Indian cuisine can easily be adjusted to suit the tastes of both cook and guests. Even without excessive use of chili peppers and other hot spices, Indian cooking is still unexcelled in aroma and flavor.

Indian cooking has steadily gained popularity in the Western world not just because of the delicious flavors of its dishes, but also because of the general healthfulness of its cuisine. The abundant use of vegetables, rice, and legumes makes the dishes very nutritious and low in fat and sugar. The recipes are so delicious, in fact, that one can easily pursue a vegetarian lifestyle without missing the flavors of meat-based dishes. I hope you will want to cook many complete Indian meals using the recipes contained in this cookbook, but I would also urge you to incorporate some of these dishes (appetizers, vegetables, rice, and breads) into a traditional Western meal. If you do so, I am confident that you will find your meals greeted with renewed enthusiasm by family members and guests alike.

I feel privileged to have had the opportunity of working so closely with Alamelu in helping to record her recipes, which have come from a long tradition of South Indian cooking. In writing down these recipes to pass along to new generations of cooks, I have had the joy of private tutoring from a talented and wonderfully generous cook. I would urge you to give the recipes a try and to embark yourself upon a culinary adventure which you will never regret. Happy cooking!

Patricia Marquardt

September, 1997

About the Author

Patricia Marquardt is a tenured Associate Professor of Classical Languages at Marquette University in Milwaukee, Wisconsin. Her academic degrees, all in the area of Ancient Greek and Latin Philology, include a B.A. from Ripon College, a M.A. from the University of Chicago, and a Ph.D. from the University of Wisconsin-Madison. A native of Milwaukee, Patricia has also taught at Mt. Mary College and the University of Wisconsin, Milwaukee. She curently heads the Classical Languages Program at Marquette University. She has published numerous scholarly articles in the areas of Classical Mythology, Homer, and Archaic Greek Poetry.

Dehli

Calcutta

Mumbai
(Bombay)

Bay of
Bengal

ANDHRA PRADESH

Arabian
Sea

KARNATAKA

Bangalore

Chennai
(Madras)

Mysore

India

KERALA

TAMIL NADU

Cochin

Madurai

Trivandrum

Indian Ocean

A Glimpse of South India

The term "South India" usually refers to the southern peninsula of the vast Indian subcontinent made up of the four states: Tamil Nadu and Andhra Pradesh on the east coast, Karnataka and Kerala on the west coast. South Indian people from these states have distinct cultural characteristics and speak different languages Tamil, Telegu, Kannada and Malayalam respectively. These languages have rich and well established literatures with Tamil being the most ancient of them. An important common feature of the South Indians is their Dravidian origin in contrast to the predominantly Aryan origin of the people of the North. The vast majority of South Indians are Hindus, but Muslims and Christians form sizeable minorities and have also made significant contributions in the South. Since historically the northern part of India bore the brunt of foreign invasions, South India has been affected less by the resulting influences. Thus the culture and religious practices, as well as the food, of the South tend to reflect long-standing traditions.

South Indian geographical features include hill-ranges, beautiful plateaus, dusty hot plains, rivers and sea-coasts populated by a large number of villages, small towns and many cosmopolitan cities. Two of the premier cities of South India are Chennai (formerly known as Madras) in Tamil Nadu and Bangalore in Karnataka. Both of these cities have large industrial complexes, extensive cultural activities, centers of state governments and highly regarded academic institutions. Because of its high-tech industries, Bangalore has come to be known as the Silicon Valley of India, and has attracted numerous multi-national corporations. While Madras is on the coast that borders the Indian ocean and has a tropical climate, Bangalore is located about 200 miles to the west on the Deccan plateau and has a moderate climate. Interestingly, from the perspective of our cookbook, both cities boast of an exquisite variety of South Indian foods.

Other areas in the South noted for their outstanding cuisines include the Chettinad region and the ancient cities of Tanjore and Madurai in Tamil Nadu; Udupi and Mysore in Karnataka; Cochin and Trivandrum in Kerala; and Hyderabad in Andhra Pradesh. Chettinad, the land of the Chettiars, is a region located about 250 miles south of Madras. The Chettiar community was historically known for its banking and business achievements, wealth, charitable pursuits and hospitality. Chettinad cooking has always been distinctive, and recently has become especially popular in Madras and in many other cities of South India. Chettinad cuisine is characterized by thick and delicious sauces such as kulambu and a dry stir-fry style of cooking vegetarian and non-vegetarian dishes called poriyal. This cusine is also known for its wide variety of unique savories and sweets called palakaram served usually at breakfast, tea-time and the evening meal. Chettinad cooking techniques have influenced the cuisines of many other parts of South India. Conversely, other parts of South India, in particular Kerala and Karnataka, have influenced Chettinad cooking. While most of the foods we have presented in this book can be found in the various regions of South India, many of our recipes have their roots in the rich cooking tradition of Chettinad, the native region of one of the authors of this book.

SPICES AND OTHER BASICS

With very few exceptions, spices used in South Indian cooking can be found in most American supermarkets. The spices not found in local supermarkets can be obtained from Indian and Oriental grocery stores. One can also mail order spices from many Indian grocery stores in the U.S. and in Canada.

Spices Used in South Indian Cooking

Asafoetida (Hing) - A rare spice with a strong aroma. It is used in very small quantities in some vegetarian and rice dishes. It is available in lump, or powdered form. The Powdered form, available in Indian grocery stores, is recommended.

Black Mustard Seeds - Small round black seeds. Mustard seeds are often used in combination with urad dal in vegetarian, rice, and sambhar dishes.

Black pepper (Peppercorns or Mirchi) - Used whole or in powdered form. Powdered black pepper and cumin, mixed in equal portion, can be used in chicken curry, over fried eggs and in yogurt salads to add a wonderful taste. The combination of black pepper and cumin powder in soups and rasam is believed to be an effective remedy for colds.

Cardamom (Elaichi) - A highly aromatic spice used primarily to flavor tea, soup and dessert dishes. The seed may be used whole or in powdered form. Cardamom is also used as a breath freshener.

Coconut - Widely used as a garnish for cooked vegetables and as a base for kurmas and chutneys. Fresh coconut is available in general grocery stores. Electric mini choppers may be used to shred fresh coconut. Shredded unsweetened coconut is also available in Indian grocery stores. The milk of the coconut is not often used in Indian cooking, but it is used as a refreshing beverage on a hot summer day.

Coriander - An aromatic herb which may be purchased as leaves, seeds or powder. Also called cilantro in Spanish and Mexican recipes, it is used both as a seasoning, and as a garnish. Coriander chutney is a very popular accompaniment to vadas, idli and dosas.

Cumin (Jeera) - Commonly used in whole or powdered form. Powdered cumin, in combination with black pepper, is used over fried eggs, soups and yogurt dishes.

Fennel Seeds - Larger in size than cumin. Commonly used in non-vegetarian cooking and in soups. Roasted fennel seeds are used as a breath freshener after meals.

Fenugreek (methi) - Small brown seeds which are bitter tasting. Used sparingly in non-vegetarian dishes such as seafood.

Ginger - A root-spice that is often used in Indian cooking. Ginger with garlic paste is a popular combination that adds a wonderful flavor to any dish. Ginger also aids in digestion. Ginger is available in powdered form, but fresh ginger is highly recommended for its flavor and healthfulness.

Green Chilies - A common ingredient which imparts a spicy, hot flavor to many Indian dishes. Chilies come in a wide variety, and you may use any of the many types available. Chilies may be used sparingly or omitted entirely depending on your taste.

Saffron - An expensive and highly aromatic spice which adds flavor and color to rice and meat dishes. Saffron is also used widely in desserts.

Tamarind (imli) - Tamarind is a bean with a sweet and sour taste which adds a certain tartness to dishes. Bottled tamarind paste is available in Indian grocery stores. Lemon juice may be substituted for tamarind.

Turmeric Powder (haldi) - A yellow root-spice that has been dried and powdered. A natural food coloring which imparts a bright yellow color to any dish. Reportedly turmeric paste is good for the complexion.

Urad dal - A lentil that can be used whole or split. When urad dal is fried, it becomes crunchy and has a nutty taste. Available in Indian grocery stores.

KEY INGREDIENTS
in South Indian Cooking

Basmati Rice

Basmati rice - Basamati is a fragrant, high quality rice used in making certain rice dishes. Available in Indian grocery stores. The grains of Basmati are finer than the grains of other rices and they separate beautifully after they are cooked. Basmati rice is unexcelled for making pulaoo and flavored rice dishes.

Dhall (DAL)

Dals are legumes rich in protein which provide the base for vegetarian dishes.

Channa dal - A kind of lentil that is yellow in color. When roasted, it has a nutty and crunchy taste. Used in making vada and kootu dishes.

Masoor dal - An orange colored lentil used in making sambhars. Masoor dal, which cooks faster than toor dal, can be substituted for Toor dal in sambhars and other recipes.

Toor (or) Toovar dal - a kind of lentil that looks very similar to split peas. Used as a creamy base in making sambhars.

Urad dal - A lentil that is rich in protein and iron and can be used whole or split. Urad dal may be used both as a seasoning and as a base for vada, idli and dosa.

Curry and Masala Powders

Black Pepper and Cumin Powder - Combine both spices in equal portion and grind coarsely. Delicious when sprinkled on meat dishes and on fried eggs. (Homemade).

Curry Powder - Ingredients are coriander, fenugreek, turmeric, cumin, black pepper, bay leaves, cloves, red pepper and ginger. Used in both vegetarian and non-vegetarian dishes. Available in regular supermarkets.

Garam Masala Powder - Mixture of coriander seed powder, cumin powder, cinnamon, cloves, black pepper and cardamom powder. It is used for cooking vegetables, meat dishes, dals, pulaoo and curry dishes. Available in Indian grocery stores.

Homemade Masala Powder - Roast and grind 2 cups of whole red chili peppers with 1 cup of coriander seed. Grind to a fine powder and store in an air-tight bottle for use as necessary. Ready-made Sambhar powders are also good.

Poodhi Powder - Roast and grind 1 cup of red chili peppers with $\frac{1}{2}$ cup of urad dal, half teaspoon asafoetida, and half teaspoon salt. Grind the mixture coarsely. Used as an accompaniment to idli, dosa and as a seasoning in vegetable dishes. Ready-made Poodhi powder is sold in Indian grocery stores as chutney powder and is equally good as the homemade powder.

Rasam Powder - Mixture of coriander seed powder, red pepper and cumin powder, fenugreek powder, curry leaves and asafoetida. Available in Indian grocery stores.

Red Pepper(Cayenne) Powder - Available in regular and specialty grocery stores. Commonly used in both vegetarian and non-vegetarian recipes.

Sambhar Powder - Combination of turmeric powder, cumin powder, red pepper powder, asafoetida and coriander seeds. Available in Indian grocery stores.

Vindaloo Curry Paste - Ingredients in this paste are coriander, cumin, turmeric, red pepper, salt, ginger, garlic, tamarind and some vegetable oil. Available in jars at Indian grocery stores for a small price.

SOME GENERAL TIPS
for Cooking South Indian Dishes

❏ Buy spices in small quantities to maintain freshness.

❏ In South Indian cooking you do not have to be too precise in measuring your spices. If you add a little more or less of the ingredients than the amount specified in the recipe, you are not going to spoil the preparation. Most cooks in South India do not use measuring cups or spoons.

❏ Before preparing a dish, read the recipe carefully and assemble all the ingredients that will be needed to make the dish.

❏ The basic utensils recommended for South Indian cooking are the following: small, medium and large stainless steel saucepans; cast-iron skillets and non-stick skillets; a regular or electric wok; spice grinder; food processor; electric blender; rice cooker and pressure cooker.

❏ When cooking rice dishes, cook the rice in a regular saucepan or in a rice cooker. Transfer cooked rice to a large bowl and let it cool. Then, make the flavored rice dish in a regular or electric wok. It is important that the rice grains be separate to make a good flavored rice dish. Always wash the Basmati rice before cooking.

❏ In Indian cooking, you can make all your dishes ahead of time except for the bread. Just before dinner, you can heat up each dish in a microwave oven. Indian food, once prepared, can be kept in the refrigerator or freezer and can be reheated   later without loss of flavor.

❏ Cooking dal in a pressure cooker is efficient and quite safe if you follow manufacturer's instructions not to fill pressure cooker over half full and not to open pressure cooker until the air vent/ cover lock has dropped and pressure is completely reduced.

❏ Besides cooking dal in a pressure cooker as indicated in the recipes, you may also cook dal in a   saucepan or in a microwave using the following instructions:

Cooking Dal in a Saucepan: Bring water to a boil in a saucepan. Add dal and turmeric powder as indicated in the recipe. Cook dal uncovered until it becomes creamy. If you cover dal while cooking, it may bubble up and overflow the saucepan. Watch that water does not totally evaporate. While cooking dal, generously keep adding water to dal in saucepan until the dal is thoroughly cooked. *If you do not have the time to use Toor dal to make sambhar, you may substitute Masoor dal which cooks in less than half the time of Toor dal.*

Cooking Dal in a Microwave: Soak the specified amount of dal for one hour in enough water to cover the dal thoroughly. Place dal with water in a microwave-safe dish. Cook uncovered in a carousel microwave oven on high heat for one hour. Check every 15 minutes and, if necessary, add additional water until dal becomes creamy.

❑ Most of the recipes included in this book serve 4 to 6 people. However, the number of the servings depends upon the size of the helping. Recipes can always be increased proportionately when necesary.

❑ Unsweetened coconut powder, available in Indian grocery stores, can be substituted for fresh coconut. The unsweetened coconut powder can be used as garnish and also as a base for making chutneys and kurma.

Appetizers

Beet Vadas

Bhajis

Bondas

Marinated Chicken Masala

Pakoras

Pappadums

Samosas

Stuffed Mushrooms

Tandoori Chicken Delights

Tuna Balls

Vegetable Cutlets

Beet Vadas
(Fried Vegetable Patties)

These delicious treats may be served as appetizers or as an accompaniment to a meal.

1 cup yellow split peas
3 or 4 whole red chili peppers
$\frac{3}{4}$ teaspoon whole cumin
$\frac{1}{2}$ teaspoon fennel seeds
$\frac{1}{2}$ cup finely shredded raw beets
$\frac{3}{4}$ cup diced yellow onion
$\frac{1}{2}$ cup chopped coriander
1 teaspoon minced fresh ginger (optional)
1 to 2 green chili peppers (optional)
$\frac{1}{2}$ teaspoon salt
1 to $1\frac{1}{2}$ cups dry bread crumbs
corn oil for frying

❑ Soak yellow split peas in approximately 2 cups of water for 2 to 3 hours. Drain split peas and grind them in a blender to a coarse texture (similar to corn meal). Add red chilies, cumin and fennel seeds to blender and grind along with split peas. Grind about $\frac{1}{2}$ cup of soaked split peas at a time with only enough water added each time to facilitate the grinding process. Do not grind the split peas too finely. It is desirable to have a few whole split peas in the mixture to lend a crunchy texture to the finished vadas.

❑ Remove the split pea mixture from blender and place in a large bowl. Use your hand to blend the mixture of split peas and spices thoroughly.

❑ Add the beets, onion, coriander, ginger, green chilies and salt to the mixture. Blend thoroughly by hand.

❑ Add bread crumbs to the mixture and blend by hand until mixture reaches a consistency sufficiently thick to form a ball. Slightly more than $1\frac{1}{2}$ cups of bread crumbs may be needed if the mixture is too watery.

❑ Take a small portion of mixture (about 1 tablespoon) in the palm of the hand and form into a ball. With fingers, flatten ball into the shape of a small patty, either in the palm of the hand or on a small plate. The patty should be about 1 inch in diameter.

❏ Fry a few vadas at a time in about ¼ inch of corn oil until golden brown. Remove vadas from hot oil with a perforated spatula and drain them on paper towels. Repeat the procedure until the desired number of vadas has been made. **Note:** Any unused mixture may be refrigerated for further use. Use the refrigerated mix within a day or two.

Variations: A number of different vegetables may be substituted for the shredded beets in the basic recipe. These include 1½ cups of chopped fresh spinach; 1½ cups of chopped and slightly cooked cabbage and ⅔ cup of shredded raw carrots. If using the spinach or cabbage, be certain to blend the vegetables thoroughly into the split pea mixture. Simple onion vadas may be made by following the basic recipe and doubling the amount of chopped onions from ¾ cup to 1½ cups.

Makes 40 small vadas.

Bhajis
(Vegetable Fritters)

1 cup chickpea flour
¼ cup rice flour
1 teaspoon salt
1 to   2 teaspoons fresh red chili powder
1 tablespoon all purpose flour
½ teaspoon powdered asafoetida
¼ teaspoon turmeric powder
sliced potatoes w/skins (¼" thick)
sliced onion (¼" thick)

❑ Mix together all of the dry ingredients by hand.

❑ Add approximately ½ cup of water to make a smooth, thick batter.

❑ Coat the potato or onion slices by dipping them in the batter. Fry slices in a cast iron skillet in about ½ of corn oil. Fry until golden brown on both sides (about 3 to 4 minutes).

❑ Drain on paper towels and serve warm with chutney or by themselves.

Note: Instant pakora mix may be purchased and used in place of the above various dry ingredients.

Makes 24 bhajis.

Bondas

Bondas are deep fried dumplings made with potatoes and mixed vegetables dipped in a batter of chickpea flour.

For Filling:

4 Idaho potatoes (medium sized)
¾ teaspoon turmeric powder (divided)
1 teaspoon salt (divided)
1 large onion, chopped
1 teaspoon minced ginger
½ tomato, chopped
1 green chili pepper, chopped
1 tablespoon corn oil
½ teaspoon asafoetida powder
1 teaspoon mustard seeds
1½ teaspoon urad dal
1 teaspoon lemon juice
½ cup chopped coriander (cilantro)

For Batter:

1½ cups Besan flour (chickpea flour)
½ cup rice flour
1 teaspoon chilipowder (red pepper powder)
½ teaspoon salt
½ teaspoon asafoetida powder
About 2 cups corn oil for frying

❏ Scrub potatoes. Cut in half and place in pressure cooker. Add enough water to cover potatoes together with ½ teaspoon turmeric powder and ½ teaspoon salt. Cover and cook (about 10 minutes) until potatoes are tender. (Take note of the manufacturer's safety instructions when using a pressure cooker. If you prefer not to use a pressure cooker, you may use any uncovered saucepan to boil the potoatoes.)

❏ Chop onion, ginger, tomato, and green chilies. Set aside.

❏ Remove skins from potatoes and mash potatoes coarsely.

❑ Pour 1 tablespoon of corn oil in skillet. When oil is hot but not smoking, add asafoetida, mustard seeds and urad dal. Cover and fry until mustard seeds pop and urad dal is golden brown.

❑ Add chopped onion, ginger, tomato and chilies to skillet. Stir fry for a few minutes. Add ¼ teaspoon turmeric powder, ½ teaspoon salt and 1 teaspoon lemon juice.

❑ Add mashed potatoes and stir well. Add ½ cup of chopped coriander to potatoes and mix well. Set aside until batter is prepared.

Ready made pakora mix may be used or you may make the batter as follows:

❑ Mix together all dry ingredients.

❑ Pour warm water over dry ingredients to form a thick and smooth paste. (Note: batter must be thick so add only a little water at a time.)

❑ Shape the potato mixture into balls and coat balls with batter. Fry the coated balls in corn oil until golden brown.

Makes 24 bondas. Serve with chutney.

Marinated Chicken Masala (Baked or Grilled)

3 to 4 boneless, skinless chicken breast fillets
2 thin slices of fresh ginger
½ onion, sliced
2 teaspoons cumin seeds
3 green chili peppers
2 to 3 garlic cloves
¼ cup chopped coriander
¼ cup corn oil or olive oil
¾ teaspoon plain or garlic salt

❏ Cut chicken fillets into small pieces.

❏ Grind ginger, onion, cumin seeds, chilies, garlic cloves, and coriander with oil.

❏ Pour marinade (ground mixture) over chicken pieces in a small bowl.

❏ Add salt. Cover chicken tightly with saran wrap and refrigerate for 24 hours.

❏ Bake chicken at 350 degrees for 20 minutes on a baking pan or grill chicken for 20 minutes.

May be served as an appetizer or as a main meal with rice and vegetables.

Makes 20 to 24 pieces.

Pakoras
(Vegetable Fritters)

2 cups chick pea flour (Besan)
¼ cup rice flour
1 teaspoon salt
¼ teaspoon asafoetida powder
1 large onion, chopped (more if desired)
½ cup of cashew halves
1 green chili pepper, chopped (more if desired)
1 bell pepper, chopped (optional)
½ cup chopped coriander
corn oil for deep frying (approximately 2")

❑ Mix flours, salt, and asafoetida with 2 cups of cold water. Use your hand to blend the ingredients into a smooth batter.

❑ Add onion, cashews, green chili, bell pepper, and coriander to batter. Batter should be very thick and should coat the vegetables thoroughly.

❑ Heat corn oil in a skillet or frying pan. When oil is hot, but not smoking, drop spoonfuls of batter into oil and fry until golden brown.

Serve as an appetizer with chutney.

Note: Instant pakora mix may be purchased and used in place of the above various dry ingredients.

Makes 20 to 24 pakoras.

Pappadums

Pappadums, (Appalam as they are called in the South) can be bought in Indian grocery stores. There are several varieties of the pappadum, which is essentially a wafer made from urad dal. Pappadums can be deep-fried in hot oil and served as appetizers or as an accompaniment to meals. The frying takes just a few seconds. For convenience, the large ones can be broken into half and then fried.

10 pappadums
oil for deep frying, about 2" in a skillet

❑ Set a large platter, lined with paper towels, beside the stove to drain the pappadums.

❑ Heat oil in skillet over medium heat.

❑ When oil is hot, but not smoking put one pappadum in skillet.

❑ As the oil sizzles the pappadum will expand.

❑ Turn pappadum over once and remove in a few seconds with slotted spoon.

❑ Prepare as many pappadum as you like but fry only one at a time. Allow one pappadum per person.

Variation: Place one pappad in the microwave. Cook pappad on high for 1 to 1½ minutes. Serve pappad as an appetizer or with meal. (Pappad served without deep frying).

Samosas

Six ready-made, small flour tortillas
Filling for samosas (potato curry, tuna curry, or ground beef
and split peas—*see index*)

❑ Warm tortillas slightly in plastic wrap in microwave for 30 seconds.

❑ Cut tortillas in half and moisten the halves with water.

❑ Holding one half of the tortilla in palm of a hand, fold it into a cone shape by bringing the two ends of the tortilla together.

❑ Put one teaspoon of filling into cone, being careful not to over fill. Moisten top edges of cone and fold down to seal tightly.

❑ Deep fry in corn oil over low heat until golden brown.

❑ Set the fried samosas on a paper towel to drain excess oil.

Serve samosas with any kind of chutney.

Samosas can also be prepared from scratch using all purpose flour for shells. Recipe follows:

1 cup all purpose flour
¼ teaspoon salt
¼ cup of oil

❑ Mix together all the above ingredients with fingers, adding only enough water to form a soft dough.

❑ Allow the dough to settle for one hour at room temperature before filling with mixture.

❑ Divide the dough into small, smooth balls. Roll each ball into a circular shape. Moisten edges and fold into a cone shape as with tortillas. Fill with stuffing mixture and seal edges before frying.

Makes 10 to 12 small samosas

Stuffed Mushrooms

24 mushroom caps
spinach poriyal (see p. 158) or tuna masala (see p. 38)
2 tablespoons butter

❑ Wash and dry mushrooms. Remove stems and hollow out mushroom pulp to form cups.

❑ Fill mushroom cups with spinach poriyal or tuna masala.

❑ Dot filled mushrooms with butter and bake uncovered (or lightly tented on a greased cooking sheet) at 400 degrees (preheated oven) for 15 to 20 minutes.

Makes 24 stuffed mushrooms.

Tandoori Chicken Delights

4 boneless, skinless chicken breasts, cut into small pieces
bottled tandoori paste (available in Indian grocery stores)
2 tablespoons melted butter
chopped coriander, for garnish

❑ Marinate the chicken in about 1 teaspoon tandoori paste for 4 to 6 hours.

❑ Place chicken slices on a cookie sheet and brush with melted butter. Bake at 350 degrees for about 15 to 20 minutes (until tender).

❑ Sprinkle with chopped coriander and serve with toothpicks. Instead of baking the chicken one may also grill the chicken for 15 to 20 minutes.

Makes 20 to 24 chicken delights.

Tuna Balls

3 tablespoons corn oil
2 to 3 very small pieces of cinnamon stick
$\frac{1}{4}$ teaspoon fennel seeds
$\frac{1}{4}$ teaspoon cumin seeds
1 teaspoon urad dal
1 cup chopped yellow onions
$\frac{1}{4}$ cup finely chopped tomato
$\frac{1}{4}$ cup minced garlic
2 green chili peppers (more if desired)
$\frac{1}{4}$ cup minced coriander
$\frac{1}{4}$ teaspoon turmeric powder
2 teaspoons curry powder
$\frac{1}{4}$ cup tomato sauce
1 ($9\frac{1}{4}$ oz.) can tuna in oil
$\frac{1}{2}$ teaspoon salt
1 egg
$\frac{3}{4}$ cup plain bread crumbs

❑ Pour corn oil into a cast-iron skillet over medium heat. When oil is hot, but not smoking add cinnamon stick, fennel seeds, cumin and urad dal.

❑ When urad dal is golden add the chopped onions, tomato, garlic, green chili pepper and coriander. Cook for one minute. Add turmeric, curry powder and tomato sauce. Mix and cook for another minute.

❑ Add tuna and mix thoroughly with other ingredients and cook for another minute or two. Set mixture aside on the counter and allow to cool.

❑ Add 1 egg and the bread crumbs to the tuna mixture. Mix together with hand or with a spoon. Add sufficient bread crumbs for mixture to form a ball. You may need to add more than the stated amount of bread crumbs if the tuna mixture is too watery.

❑ Form the tuna mixture into small tuna balls (about 1 inch in diameter) and deep fry in corn oil until golden brown on all sides (about 2 minutes). Fry about 6 to 8 balls at a time.

❑ Drain on paper towel and serve either warm or cold. May be reheated in microwave before serving.

Delicious Variation: To make tuna masala poriyal follow the above recipe through to the third step, then add $\frac{1}{4}$ cup of seasoned (Italian) bread crumbs to the tuna mixture. Stir fry for 5 minutes in cast-iron skillet. Tuna masala may be used as a side-dish with rice or with any bread. It may also be used as a sandwich filling or over cocktail rye as an appetizer.

Makes 24 to 30 tuna balls.

Vegetable Cutlets

4 small Idaho potatoes
1 teaspoon salt
½ teaspoon turmeric powder
2 green chili peppers
 2 tablespoons chopped coconut
1 to 2 slices of fresh ginger
1 clove garlic
¼ teaspoon cumin seeds
¼ teaspoon fennel
1 small piece of cinnamon
1 whole clove
¼ cup beets
1 onion, chopped
¼ cup chopped coriander
¼ cup frozen green peas
1 cup rice flour
½ cup water
1 to 2 cups plain bread cumbs

❏ Cut potatoes in half and place in pressure cooker with ½ teaspoon salt, turmeric powder and enough water to cover potatoes. Cook until tender, about 10 minutes (Take note of the manufacturer's safety instructions when using a pressure cooker.). Potatoes may also be cooked in a regular, uncovered kettle. When potatoes are tender, mash and set aside.

❏ Put chilies, coconut, ginger, garlic, cumin, fennel, cinnamon, and the clove into blender with ¼ cup water. Blend to a thick paste. Slightly more water may be needed to facilitate the blending process.

❏ Grate the beets.

❏ Pour one tablespoon of oil in an iron skillet over medium heat. When oil is hot but not smoking immediately add chopped onions and stir fry for about 30 seconds.

❏ Add the ground spices to skillet and stir well for 1 to 2 minutes. Add potatoes and stir well. Cook mixture over medium heat.

❏ Cook peas in microwave for one minute and then add peas to mixture in skillet. Add beets and stir well.

❑ After the vegetable and spice mixture is thoroughly mixed and heated through, remove from heat and allow to cool.

❑ Form potato mixture into small oval patties.

❑ Mix rice flour with water to create a thick batter.

❑ Dip potato patties into rice flour batter and roll in plain bread crumbs.

❑ Deep fry patties until golden brown and crisp.

Serve vegetable cutlets plain or with chutney.

Variation:

❑ Roll potato patties in cajun bread crumbs.

❑ Heat skillet with 2 to 3 teaspoons of corn oil at a time and fry 2 to 3 potato patties until golden brown and crisp.

Makes 8 to 12 cutlets.

Soups and Rasam

Cauliflower Soup

Chicken Soup

Shrimp Soup

Tomato Rasam

Pineapple Rasam

Cauliflower Soup

9 cups water (approximate)
⅓ cup toor dal
1 teaspoon turmeric powder (divided)
3 tablespoons corn oil
2 to 3 small pieces of cinnamon stick
½ bay leaf
¼ teaspoon fennel seeds
½ teaspoon cumin seeds
1 large yellow onion, cut lengthwise
1 large tomato, chopped
1 green chili pepper, finely chopped (more if desired)
⅓ cup fresh coriander, finely chopped
½ cup tomato sauce
2 teaspoons salt
½ teaspoon cardamom powder
1 small head cauliflower, in 1½" florets

❑ Cook dal in one of the suggested ways (see p. 23-24). If using pressure cooker, pour 2 cups of water into pressure cooker. In a small round cake pan, which fits neatly in bottom of pressure cooker, add toor dal, ½ teaspoon turmeric powder, and 1 cup of water. Cook 15 minutes in pressure cooker. (Take note of manufacturer's safety instructions when using a pressure cooker.) After cooking, set aside the dal mixture. Do not drain water from dal.

❑ Pour corn oil into tall saucepan and heat over medium heat. When oil is hot, but not smoking, add cinnamon stick, bay leaf, fennel and cumin seeds. Stir quickly. Cover and heat until seeds are golden brown (about 30 seconds).

❑ Add chopped onion, tomato, green chili, coriander and stir. Add remaining ½ teaspoon turmeric powder. Stir well and cook uncovered until onions are tender.

❑ Add tomato sauce and cook over medium heat for another 2 to 3 minutes. The above mixture may be mashed slightly with a spoon or with a masher to obtain a creamier consistency while cooking.

❑ Add the dal mixture from pressure cooker (about 2 cups) and 6 additional cups of warm water. Be certain to mash the dals or work them with the fingers until they are creamy before adding them to the saucepan. If water has evaporated from the dal mixture in the pressure cooker, add enough warm water to dal to make 2 cups of creamy mixture.

❑ Add salt and cardamom powder to saucepan. Stir well. Cook uncovered over medium heat until mixture begins to boil.

❑ Add cauliflower and cook uncovered until just tender (about 2 minutes). Be careful not to overcook cauliflower.

❑ If desired, you may add additional chopped coriander as a garnish.

❑ Remove from heat. Serve immediately or cover and briefly reheat before serving.

Variation: Instead of cauliflower, you may also use beets or carrots or tomatoes in the above recipe.

Makes 6 to 8 cups.

Chicken Soup

9 cups water (approximate)
$\frac{1}{4}$ cup toor dal, cooked to a creamy consistency
5 to 6 chicken thighs with bones (about $2\frac{1}{2}$ lbs.) or
   boneless, skinless chicken thighs
$1\frac{1}{2}$ tablespoons corn oil
1 bay leaf, broken
2 small pieces of cinnamon stick
$\frac{1}{2}$ teaspoon cumin seeds
$\frac{1}{2}$ teaspoon fennel seeds
1 onion, cut lengthwise
3 cloves garlic, cut lengthwise
1 tomato, chopped
2 or 3 1 to   inch pieces of ginger, sliced
1 green chili pepper, chopped
$\frac{1}{2}$ teaspoon turmeric powder
1 teaspoon curry powder
$\frac{1}{4}$ cup fresh chopped coriander (cilantro)
1 clove garlic, crushed
1 teaspoon cumin and black pepper powder

❑ Cook dal to a creamy consistency in a pressure cooker or microwave oven. (See p. 23-24. Take note of the manufacturer's safety instructions when using a pressure cooker.)

❑ Remove chicken skin and fat. Cut chicken into small pieces.

❑ Pour corn oil into a tall saucepan. When oil is hot, but not smoking, add bay leaf, cinnamon stick, cumin and fennel. Immediately add chopped onions, garlic, tomato, ginger, and green chili. Stir for a few seconds until onions are tender.

❑ Add chicken and stir fry with onions over medium heat. Add turmeric powder and curry powder. Stir well and cook, uncovered, for 3 to 5 minutes. Add salt.

❑ Add toor dal mixture and 6 to 8 cups of warm water to chicken.

❑ Add chopped coriander and allow the soup to come to a boil. Add the crushed garlic, cumin and black pepper powder. Stir well.

❏ After soup has come to a boil, reduce heat and allow to simmer until the chicken is tender. Stir frequently. If soup thickens, add enough water to thin it. When chicken is cooked, remove from heat.

Serve this soup before dinner or over rice as a main course.

Makes 6 to 8 cups.

Shrimp Soup

1 tomato (medium-sized), coarsely chopped
¼ cup tomato sauce
1 teaspoon cumin and black pepper powder
1 teaspoon salt
¼ cup scallions, chopped
¼ teaspoon chopped fresh ginger (optional)
1 green chili pepper, chopped
1 tablespoon corn oil
2 cloves garlic, chopped
½ lb. fresh shrimp, peeled and cleaned
¼ teaspoon turmeric powder
¼ cup chopped fresh coriander (cilantro)

❑ Boil 6 cups of water. Add chopped tomato and cook until tender.

❑ Add tomato sauce, cumin and black pepper powder and salt. Stir well.

❑ Add chopped scallions, ginger and green chili.

❑ Brown garlic and shrimp in corn oil. Add turmeric powder and continue to brown for 3 to 5 minutes.

❑ When shrimp is browned, add to tomato mixture. Stir and simmer for another 2 minutes.

❑ Garnish with coriander.

Makes 4 to 6 cups.

Tomato Rasam

A thin peppery soup.

> **4 cups of water (approximate)**
> **1 small tomato, chopped**
> **½ teaspoon fresh ginger, minced**
> **¼ cup fresh coriander, chopped**
> **½ green chili pepper, minced**
> **1½ teaspoon rasam powder**
> **½ teaspoon cumin and black pepper powder**
> **1 clove garlic, crushed**
> **1 cup tomato sauce**
> **½ teaspoon salt, more if desired**
> **1 teaspoon coconut powder**

❏ Boil 4 cups of water. When water is at the point of boiling, add chopped tomato.

❏ Add chopped fresh ginger, coriander and green chili.

❏ Stir rasam powder and cumin and black pepper powder into boiling water.

❏ Crush the garlic clove and add to water with one cup of tomato sauce. Add salt and stir well.

❏ Let the ingredients simmer for about 3 minutes.

❏ Add coconut powder.

Serve hot before dinner as a soup or over rice at dinner. Also, note that the ingredients may be added in any order after the water is boiling. Rasam is an excellent remedy for colds and sore throats.

Makes 4 to 6 cups.

Pineapple Rasam

A thin peppery soup.

> ¼ cup toor dal, cooked to a creamy consistency in 1 cup of
> water
> 1 tomato, chopped
> ¼ cup fresh coriander leaves, chopped
> 1½ teaspoon rasam powder
> 1 teaspoon salt

For Garnish:

> 1 teaspoon oil
> 1 dried red pepper
> ½ teaspoon mustard seeds
> ½ teaspoon cumin seeds
> ⅓ cup fresh pineapple chunks

❑ Pour dal mixture into saucepan with 4 cups of water.

❑ Add chopped tomato and coriander. Cook until the tomato is tender.

❑ Add rasam powder and salt. Allow to boil for a minute or two.

❑ Heat oil in a butter warmer or small skillet with red pepper. When
oil is hot, but not smoking, add mustard seeds and cumin. When
mustard seeds pop, pour ingredients into rasam mixture.

Thus far, the recipe has produced dal rasam. You may also make
pineapple rasam by adding ⅓ cup of fresh pineapple to the rasam
mixture. Allow to simmer for 5 minutes before serving.

Lemon Rasam: Instead of pineapples, one may also add freshly
squeezed lemon juice (about 2 tablespoons). Allow to simmer for 5
minutes before serving. Garnish with coriander leaves.

Milagu Rasam (cumin and black pepper): Instead of pineapple or
lemon juice, one may also add about ¾ tablespoon of a freshly ground
black pepper and cumin powder to rasam mixture. Allow to simmmer
for 5 minutes. Garnish with coriander leaves.

Makes 4 to 6 cups.

Breads

Aadai

Chappati

Idiyappam

Idli

Masala Dosai

Poori

Uppuma

Urad Dal Vadai

Aadai

Thick pancake made with lentils, rice and spices.

½ cup urad dal
½ cup yellow split peas
½ cup toor dal
½ cup moong dal
1 cup extra long grain rice
4 red chili peppers
1 teaspoon cumin
1 teaspoon fennel
½ cup ground fresh coconut
½ teaspoon asafoetida powder
1 teaspoon salt
1 cup chopped onion
¼ cup chopped fresh coriander

❏ Soak the urad dal, split peas, toor dal, moong dal, and rice with red pepper and cumin for 3 hours. Grind the above to a coarse paste in the blender.

❏ Add fresh coconut, asafoetida, salt, onions and chopped coriander to the ground mixture.

❏ Mix all the ingredients well and follow the instructions as given for dosai.

❏ Any type of chutney could be served with aadai.

Serves 2 to 4 people.

Chappati

Thin, flat wheat bread.

2 cups chappati flour (wheat flour)
1 cup all-purpose white flour
½ teaspoon salt
1 tablespoon vegetable shortening
1½ cups warm water (approximate)
Corn oil for cooking

❏ Place the chappati flour and all purpose flour in a large mixing bowl. Add salt and mix well.

❏ Add the shortening. Use a pastry cutter to blend shortening and flour mixture.

❏ Gradually add approximately 1½ cups warm water to flour mixture, all the while working the dough with the hands. Continue adding the warm water gradually until dough becomes elastic and pliable. Add more water if needed, but be careful not to make dough too sticky. (Food processor may also be used to form the dough., in which case, omit the next step.)

❏ Divide the dough into 2 small portions for ease in working. Separately beat each of the 2 portions by throwing the dough vigorously 20 times into the bowl, so that the dough becomes very soft and smooth. Note: In India, cooks set the mixing bowl on the floor and pound the dough while seated on the floor.

❏ Moisten the palms of the hands with a small amount of corn oil and work each of the two dough portions into a long sausage-like shape. Next, break off small chunks of dough from each of the portions to form balls about 1½" in diameter, roughly the size of golf balls. This recipe makes about 12 to 15 chappatis, but chappatis may be made larger or smaller, depending on preference.

❏ Dust each of the balls of dough with chappati flour and on a floured board roll out evenly into a thin, flat, circular shape, 4 to 5" in diameter. At this point, chappatis are ready for cooking.

❏ For more fluffy, flaky chappatis, however, the following step is recommended: Brush half of the rolled, circular chappati with corn oil. Fold dough over oiled half. Next, brush the other half of the folded dough with oil. Again, fold over oiled half. The dough should now be roughly triangular in shape. Dust well with additional chappati flour and roll out again evenly into a thin, flat, fan-like shape.

❏ For cooking, place chappatis, one at a time, in a nonstick, dry fry-pan over medium heat. Using a spoon, lightly dabble a small amount of corn oil around and over the top of the chappati as it cooks. Cook until chappati puffs up and brown spots appear underneath (15 to 20 seconds). Turn chappati with spatula and cook the other side. Again, lightly brush top of chappati with a small amount of corn oil. Be sparing with the oil so chappati do not become too oily. When chappati is nicely browned on both sides (another 15 to 20 seconds), remove from frypan and wrap in a clean cloth to keep it warm and soft. Repeat the process with each chappati. It is best to serve chappatis while still warm.

Makes 12 to 15 chappatis.

Idiyappam

A main dish made from rice sticks, onions and chili peppers. Often served as a breakfast item.

2 teaspoons salt
4 tablespoons corn oil (divided)
1 pound rice sticks (thin)
5 to 6 curry leaves
3 teaspoons black mustard seeds
3 teaspoons urad dal
2 onions, chopped
2 green chili peppers, chopped
¼ cup chopped fresh coriander
½ cup low-fat buttermilk

❑ Boil 6 to 8 cups of water in a large saucepan.

❑ When water is boiling vigorously, add salt, ½ teaspoon corn oil, and rice sticks. Boil uncovered for about 5 minutes. Do not overcook. Oil is added to the boiling water to prevent rice sticks from sticking together.

❑ When noodles are tender, drain thoroughly in a colander. Set aside.

❑ Place corn oil in a large skillet and heat over medium heat. When oil is hot but not smoking, add curry leaves, mustard seeds and urad dal. Cover and cook until mustard seeds pop and urad dal is golden brown.

❑ Add chopped onions and chilies to skillet.

❑ Stir fry for a few minutes.

❑ Add rice sticks to ingredients in skillet. Cut sticks into smaller pieces in skillet and mix well with onions and chilies. Reduce heat to low while mixing well.

❑ Add chopped coriander.

❑ Add buttermilk to moisten noodles slightly. Stir well and add more salt, if desired.

Serve idiyappam with sambhar or chutney for a delicious combination.

Serves 2 to 4.

Idli
(Traditional)

Idlis are like steamed rice-cakes which are served for breakfast or for brunch with various kinds of sambhar. You need an idli cooker to make idli. Idli cookers are available in Indian stores. To make traditional idlis, you need to soak and grind the following ingredients a day in advance:

4 cups extra-long grain rice
1 cup urad dal
1 cup cooked long-grain rice
4 teaspoons salt

❑ Soak rice and dal separately in water for about 6 to 8 hours.

❑ Grind the rice in a blender with enough water to make a coarse, creamy mixture. Add the cooked rice as you grind the soaked rice. Pour the rice batter into a large mixing bowl.

❑ Grind urad dal with enough water to make a creamy mixture. Be careful not to use too much water. The consistency should be smooth and creamy, but not watery.

❑ Pour urad dal mix over the rice batter. Add salt.

❑ With your hand, mix the batters and the salt thoroughly. It is important to use your hand, and not a spoon, because the warmth from the hand will aid the fermentation process of the batter.

❑ Cover the bowl and set side overnight in a warm place. Do not use direct heat.

❑ The following morning you will note that the batter has risen.

❑ Make idli with an idli cooker.

Idli cooker: A special type of vessel that is used to make idlis. It has a bottom pan to hold water and a plate insert with 5 to 7 round sections. A cloth is draped over idli plate and the batter is poured into the the steamed cloth. The vessel has a tight cover to steam cook the idlis.

Idli from Ready Made Mix

Idlis are like steamed rice cakes which are served for breakfast or for brunch with various kinds of sambhar. Plain or rave idli mix is available in Indian grocery stores. Follow the instructions on package and enjoy.

Serves 4 to 6.

Masala Dosai

These delicious thin rice pancakes constitute a typical South Indian breakfast. Pancakes are stuffed with potato curry and coconut chutney.

3 cups extra long-grain rice
½ cup urad dal
1 teaspoon whole fenugreek
½ cup cooked rice
2 ½ teaspoons salt
corn oil for roasting
Potato Masala (see page 155)
Coconut Chutney (see page 62)

❑ Soak rice, urad dal and fenugreek in enough water to cover. Soak the ingredients for about 6 to 8 hours.

❑ Drain water and place rice and dal mixture in an electric blender. Add only enough water to facilitate the grinding process. Grind rice mixture on high power for several minutes until it becomes a thick, smooth, creamy consistency. Add cooked rice a little at a time to the rice mixture as it is being ground.

❑ Pour the creamy rice batter into a large bowl. Add the salt and mix well with the hand. It is essential to use the hand for mixing, and not a spoon, because the warmth of the hand initiates the fermentation process. Cover bowl with a plate and place it overnight in a warm place. Do not use direct heat. The rice batter will begin to ferment and expand by itself, so be certain that the bowl you are using will allow the batter to at least double its volume.

❑ The next morning the expanded batter will be frothy. Beat it down with a large spoon for several minutes.

❑ Pour a large spoonful of batter into the center of a hot, non-stick skillet. Move the spoon over the batter in 3 to 4 concentric circles, starting at the inside of the circle and working toward the outside. The purpose of this step is to spread out the batter thinly and evenly. Do not go back over the circles or smear the batter. It is all right if there are small holes in the batter as it browns in the skillet. Fry over medium/high heat. As the dosai is browning well on one side, brush the top side evenly with corn oil. Cover and cook for 1 to 2 minutes. Turn dosai and brown slightly on the other side. Again, brush top side of dosai with corn oil.

❑ Turn dosai once again so browner side is on bottom. With a spoon, spread coconut chutney evenly over top side of dosai. Place 1 to 2 tablespoons of masala potato curry over coconut chutney, on one half of dosai only. Fold the dosai up over the potato mixture and pat down with a spatula. The dosai should now have a semi-circular shape.

❑ Brush top side of dosai with butter or margarine. Turn and continue browning for approximately 30 seconds. Brush bottom side of dosai with butter or margarine and likewise brown for 30 seconds.

❑ Remove dosai to serving platter as you repeat the same procedure with other dosai. Be certain to wipe all oil from skillet with a paper towel before you start making the next dosai. Otherwise the batter will not spread evenly in the skillet.

❑ A softer dosai, without stuffing, may also be prepared. For this method, follow the same instructions given above, but do not brush the dosai with oil as it browns. Cover skillet and brown on only one side. Do not turn dosai. Serve plain dosai with chutney on the side.

Serves 4 to 6.

Poori

A deep-fried wheat bread which puffs like a balloon when fried in oil.

2 cups graham wheat flour
1 cup all purpose, pre-sifted white flour
1 teaspoon salt
1 tablespoon shortening
Water (approximately 1 ¼ cups)
Corn oil for deep frying

❑ Place the first 3 dry ingredients in a large bowl and mix well by hand. Add shortening to dry ingredients and blend in thoroughly by hand.

❑ Pour lukewarm water over flour mixture a little at a time. Work dough with hand until it forms a hard dough without sticking to the fingers.

❑ Knead dough well with oiled hand. A dusting of wheat flour may be needed if dough becomes too sticky. Pound dough vigorously into bowl at least 15 times. (Food processor may also be used to form the dough.)

❑ Break off a small piece of dough and, using the palms of both hands, form a small, smooth ball, approximately 1" in diameter. If large pooris are desired, the dough should be formed into balls about about 2" in diameter.

❑ After dusting ball with a little flour, roll evenly into a circular shape, similar to a thin pancake. Keep the pooris separate, either by placing them between greaseproof paper or by dusting them with a little flour.

❑ Heat the corn oil in a wok or in an electric fry pan until a poori dropped into the oil immediately sizzles and rises to the surface. Fry the pooris one at a time. The poori should puff up and be cooked about 30 to 45 seconds. Using a slotted spoon, turn the pooris from time to time to ensure that both sides are cooked evenly. Lift out from the deep fryer, drain off the excess oil on paper towels and serve hot.

Basic recipe makes approximately 20 small pooris.

Uppuma

Cream of wheat or rice cooked with spices.

1 tablespoon corn oil
1 dried red pepper
1 teaspoon black mustard seeds
1 teaspoon urad dal
1 cup of quick or regular cream of wheat
1 teaspoon salt
¾ teaspoon red pepper powder
2 cups water
1 tablespoon margarine or butter
½ cup minced coriander leaves

❑ Pour corn oil into a skillet.

❑ When oil is hot, but not smoking, add red pepper, mustard seeds and urad dal.

❑ When urad dal turns golden, add cream of wheat and stir it for a minute or two.

❑ Add salt and red pepper powder and stir.

❑ Add water, and stir. Cover and cook on low heat, stirring frequently.

❑ Add butter or margarine. Add chopped coriander and stir well.
   Option: You may also add ½ cup of roasted cashews and mix well.

Serve uppuma with sambhar or chutney.

Tomatobath (Tomato Uppuma): Follow the same recipe as above. After adding coriander and cashews, one may also add ¼ cup chopped tomatoes. Stir well.

Vegetable Uppuma: Follow the same recipe as above. After adding water to cream of wheat, you may add about 4 oz. of frozen mixed vegetables and stir. (OR) You may add ¼ cup of shredded carrots together with ¼ cup of cooked green peas and stir. Cook and cover over low heat, stirring frequently. Add butter or margarine. Garnish with chopped coriander and cashews.

Serves 2.

Urad Dal Vadai

1 cup urad dal
1 or 2 teaspoons urad flour (optional)
1 onion, finely chopped
1 to 2 green chili peppers, finely chopped
¾ teaspoon salt
¼ cup fresh coriander, chopped
corn oil for frying

❑ Soak urad dal in generous amount of water for 2 hours.

❑ Drain water from urad dal and grind in blender to a fine, thick paste. Grind a handful of urad dal at a time with only enough water added (1 to 2 teaspoons) to facilitate the grinding process. Caution: Do not make the batter too watery; otherwise the vada will become oily when fried. If batter does become too watery, you may add 1 to 2 teaspoons or more of urad flour to thicken batter.

❑ Add finely chopped onion and green chilies to batter and mix well. The quantity of onion and chilies may be adjusted to taste.

❑ Add salt and chopped coriander to batter and mix well.

❑ Take about 1½ tablespoons of batter in hand. Form into a doughnut shape over a wet cloth and directly transfer to the hot oil. If the above method seems complicated, you may also drop batter by the spoons directly into the oil, as though making dumplings.

❑ Fry until golden brown and drain on paper towels.

Urad Vadai is delicious served with Coconut Chutney.

Makes 15 to 20 small vadai.

Chutney

Coconut Chutney I

Coconut Chutney II

Coriander Chutney I

Coriander Chutney II

Eggplant Chutney

Mint Chutney

Onion Chutney

Onion and Potato Kose

Coconut Chutney I

Chutney is a finely ground paste-like accompaniment for various appetizers.

1 coconut, cut in small pieces
½ onion, sliced
4 slices fresh ginger
2 tablespoons corn oil
½ teaspoon asafoetida powder
1 teaspoon mustard seeds
1 teaspoon urad dal
¼ cup curry leaves (optional)
¼ cup channa dal (optional)
1 teaspoon tamarind paste
8 green chili peppers, more if desired
2 to 3 teaspoons salt

❏ Cut up coconut.

❏ Slice onion and ginger.

❏ Pour oil into skillet. When oil is hot, but not smoking, add asafoetida, mustard seeds and urad dal. Cover and cook over medium heat until mustard seeds pop and urad dal is golden brown.

❏ Add all other ingredients (except salt) to skillet. Stir fry for 2 to 3 minutes.

❏ Place ingredients in a blender with as much hot water as necessary to create a smooth paste while ingredients are being processed. Grind for several minutes to a smooth paste.

❏ Add salt while grinding and adjust salt to taste.

Coconut Chutney II

1 heaping cup fresh coconut, cut in small chunks
10 green chili peppers
¼ cup chopped onion
fresh ginger
1 tablespoon channa dal
¼ teaspoon tamarind paste
2 teaspoons salt

❑ Put all ingredients in blender and add enough hot water to cover. Set blender to liquify and process for about 3 minutes. Remove chutney from blender and cool.

Note: Always keep chutneys refrigerated.

Coconut chutney is a delicious and elegant accompaniment to idli, rice dishes, chappati, and pappads.

A Delicious Variation:

1½ tablespoons corn oil
¼ teaspoon powdered asafoetida
1 dried red pepper, broken
1 teaspoon mustard seeds
1 teaspoon urad dal

❑ Heat oil, asafoetida, and red pepper over medium heat in a butter warmer or a small saucepan. When oil is hot, but not smoking, add mustard seeds and urad dal. Fry until mustard seeds burst and urad dal is golden. Pour over chutney and mix well.

Coriander Chutney I

1 teaspoon corn oil
1 teaspoon asafoetida powder
$\frac{1}{2}$ teaspoon mustard seeds
$\frac{3}{4}$ teaspoon urad dal
1 bunch of fresh coriander (washed and chopped)
6 to 8 green chili peppers (whole)
2 to 3 small slices fresh ginger
$\frac{1}{3}$ cup dried chick-peas
$\frac{1}{4}$ teaspoon tamarind paste
1 teaspoon salt (more if desired)

❏ Place oil in fry pan. When oil is hot, but not smoking, add asafoetida, mustard seeds and urad dal. Cover and fry until mustard seeds pop and urad dal is golden brown.

❏ Add chopped coriander, chilies, ginger and chick-peas. Stir fry for a few minutes.

❏ Pour all ingredients in a blender. Add tamarind paste and 1 cup hot water (enough water to grind ingredients smoothly). You may add more water if you prefer a thinner consistency.

❏ Grind until all the ingredients reach a smooth consistency. Add salt to taste.

Coriander Chutney II

Easy, delicious variation without using oil and frying.

1 bunch of fresh coriander (washed and chopped)
6 to 8 green chili peppers (more if desired)
2 to 3 small slices of fresh ginger
2 to 4 small slices of fresh coconut (optional) (or) 1
  tablespoon unsweetened coconut powder
$\frac{1}{3}$ cup dried chick-peas
$\frac{1}{4}$ teaspoon tamarind paste
1 teaspoon salt (more if desired)
1 cup hot water (more if needed)

❑ Put all above ingredients in a blender.

❑ Add hot water to grind ingredients smoothly.

❑ Add salt to taste.

Eggplant Chutney

1 small eggplant
¼ cup fresh coconut
½ tomato, chopped coarsely
6 green chili peppers (more if desired), chopped coarsely
2 to 3 red chili peppers, chopped coarsely
½ onion, chopped coarsely
2 small slices of fresh ginger
4 tablespoons corn oil (divided)
½ teaspoon asafoetida powder
1 teaspoon mustard seeds
1 teaspoon urad dal
¼ teaspoon tamarind paste
1 teaspoon salt

❏ Cut up eggplant into chunks. Do not peel eggplant.

❏ Prepare coconut, tomato, green chilies, onion, ginger and set aside.

❏ Pour 3 tablespoons corn oil into a skillet and heat until oil is hot, but not smoking. Add eggplant and fry until it becomes soft. Transfer cooked eggplant to a platter and set aside.

❏ Pour 1 tablespoon corn oil into a skillet and heat over medium heat. When the oil is hot, but not smoking, add asafoetida, mustard seeds and urad dal. Cover and fry until mustard seeds pop and urad dal is golden brown.

❏ Add coconut, chilies, ginger, onion and tomato to skillet. Stir fry for 3 to 5 minutes.

❏ Place ingredients from skillet in a blender with tamarind paste and grind coarsely. Add a small amount of water to facilitate the grinding process. Be careful not to add too much water.

❏ When ingredients are coarsely ground, add eggplant to the blender with salt and grind until eggplant is also coarsely ground.

Serve as an accompaniment to dinner or as a dip with raw vegetables, crackers, bread or chips.

Mint Chutney

1 tablespoon corn oil
¼ teaspoon asafoetida (powder)
1 teaspoon mustard seeds
1 teaspoon urad dal
2 medium onions, chopped
8 green chili peppers (more, if desired), coarsely chopped
1 cup fresh mint leaves
1 cup fresh coconut, cut into small pieces
⅓ cup dried chick-peas
¼ cup hot water (more if needed)
¼ teaspoon tamarind paste
1 teaspoon salt (more, if desired)

❑ Heat oil in a heavy skillet until hot, but not smoking. Add asafoetida powder, mustard seeds and urad dal. Cover and fry until mustard seeds pop and urad dal is golden brown.

❑ Add onion and green chilies to skillet and stir fry for a few minutes.

❑ Add mint, coconut and chick-peas to skillet and stir fry for at least 10 minutes, until the mint is cooked well.

❑ Transfer ingredients to blender and grind finely. Add ¼ cup of hot water or more to facilitate the grinding.

❑ Add tamarind paste and salt and continue grinding until ingredients reach a fine consistency.

Onion Chutney

2 ½ tablespoons corn oil (divided)
6 red chili peppers (more if desired)
1 onion, coarsely chopped
4 cloves garlic
¼ teaspoon tamarind paste
¼ teaspoon asafoetida powder
1 teaspoon mustard seeds
1 teaspoon urad dal
4 to 5 curry leaves
1 teaspoon tomato sauce
1 teaspoon salt (more if desired)

❏ Heat ½ tablespoon corn oil in an iron skillet. When oil is warm, add red peppers and fry for a minute. Remove peppers from skillet.

❏ Add onions and garlic cloves to skillet and stir fry until golden brown.

❏ Add tamarind paste and stir well into onions. Continue frying for a few minutes, while stirring. Remove from heat.

❏ Grind red peppers in blender until very fine (a powderlike consistency).

❏ Add onions and garlic to blender with ¼ to ½ cup of water.

❏ Grind on high speed until the ingredients are ground thoroughly and reach a thick consistency.

❏ Heat 2 tablespoons corn oil in skillet until hot, but not smoking. Add asafoetida, mustard seeds and urad dal, together with curry leaves. Cook, covered, until mustard seeds pop and urad dal is golden brown.

❏ Add mixture from blender with just enough water to permit the removal of onion mixture to skillet.

❏ Add tomato sauce and stir well.

❏ Add salt. Cover and continue cooking for several minutes over medium heat until the consistency becomes thicker.

This chutney is delicious with french fries, onion rings, bread or as a dip with tortilla chips. This chutney can also be served with pita or Lefse bread.

Onion and Potato Kose

2 tablespoons corn oil
2 to 4 small pieces cinnamon stick
1 bay leaf, crumbled
1 teaspoon mustard seeds
1 teaspoon urad dal
2 medium onions, chopped
1 medium tomato, chopped
2 Idaho potatoes with skins, cut in small oblong pieces
½ teaspoon turmeric powder
3 cups water
1½ cups tomato sauce
2 teaspoons salt
1 teaspoon homemade masala powder (more, if desired)
    (or) 1 teaspoon red pepper powder
¼ cup fresh coriander, minced

❑ Heat oil in a large saucepan over medium heat. When oil is hot, but not smoking, stir in cinnamon stick, bay leaf, mustard seeds and urad dal. Fry until mustard seeds burst (listen for popping sound) and urad dal is golden (about 30 seconds).

❑ Immediately add chopped onions, tomato and potatoes to saucepan. Add turmeric powder and stir well. Cook, uncovered, over medium/low heat for 1 to 2 minutes.

❑ Add water, tomato sauce, salt and masala or red pepper powder. Blend well. Add minced coriander. Cook, covered, over medium/low heat until potatoes are tender (about 8 to   10 minutes). Stir frequently.

A Delicious Variation:

In a spice grinder or coffee grinder, grind together 2 tablespoons unsweetened powdered coconut, 1 dried red pepper, ½ teaspoon fennel seeds and ½ teaspoon cumin seeds. Stir the above ground spices into cooked potato sauce. Simmer over low heat for an additional 2 to 3 minutes.

Kose is excellent with chappati, poori, idli, dosai or tortillas.

Makes 2 to 4 servings.

Rice

Basmati Rice with Green Peas

Bell Pepper and Tomato Rice

Black Pepper Rice

Coconut Rice (Carrot Rice; Apple Rice)

Lemon Rice

Sweet Pongal Rice

Tamarind Rice

Tomato Rice

Vegetable Pulaoo Rice

Yogurt Rice

Basmati Rice with Green Peas

2 cups basmati rice
4 cups hot water
2 tablespoons butter
4 to 5 small pieces cinnamon stick
2 bay leaves
1 tablespoon broken cashew nuts (more if desired)
$\frac{1}{4}$ teaspoon saffron (optional)
2 whole cloves (optional)
$\frac{1}{4}$ teaspoon turmeric powder
$\frac{1}{4}$ teaspoon ground cardamom (or 2 whole cardamoms)
$\frac{1}{2}$ teaspoon salt (more if desired)
$\frac{1}{2}$ cup frozen peas (more if desired)

❑ Wash basmati rice well and rinse thoroughly.

❑ Bring 4 cups of water to a boil in a microwave oven or on stove-top and set aside.

❑ Heat 2 tablespoons butter over medium heat in a saucepan. When butter is hot, but not smoking, add cinnamon stick, bay leaves and cashews. Fry over medium heat until cashew pieces become golden brown.

❑ Add rice to saucepan and stir well to mix all ingredients.

❑ Add saffron, cloves, turmeric powder, cardamom and salt. Mix well. Fry for a minute or two.

❑ Pour hot water over rice.

❑ Stir and wait until water with rice begins to boil.

❑ Reduce heat to low. Then cover and cook for 20 minutes or until rice is fluffy and water has evaporated.

❑ Cook green peas for 2 minutes in microwave oven until just tender. rain peas and set aside. Add peas to cooked rice before serving.

Serves 4 to 6.

Bell Pepper and Tomato Rice

2 cups basmati rice
4 cups water
4 tablespoons corn oil
4 to 5 small pieces cinnamon stick
½ bay leaf
½ teaspoon cumin seeds
½ teaspoon fennel seeds
1 large onion, cut lengthwise (divided)
1 large tomato, cut in small chunks
2 green chili peppers, finely chopped (more, if desired)
3 cups coarsely chopped green bell peppers
½ teaspoon turmeric powder
1 cup tomato sauce
1 tablespoon curry powder
2 ½ teaspoons salt
1 cup cashew halves
¼ cup butter or margarine
¼ cup onion and sage bread crumbs
¼ cup fresh coriander, minced

❑ Cook rice in 4 cups of water in a rice cooker, or cook rice in 4 cups of water following directions for fluffy rice but omitting salt and oil if included in the directions. Cool rice about one hour so grains do not stick together.

❑ Heat oil in a wok or large fry-pan over medium heat. When oil is hot, but not smoking, add cinnamon stick, bayleaf, cumin and fennel seeds. Brown for a few seconds.

❑ Add chopped onion, tomato and chilies. Stir fry for one minute.
Note: Reserve about ¼ cup of raw onion to sprinkle over finished rice.

❑ Add bell pepper and turmeric powder. Mix well.

❑ Add tomato sauce. Blend ingredients well in wok. Cook, covered, over medium heat, until bell pepper becomes slightly tender (approximately 1 minute), stirring occasionally. Do not overcook bell pepper.

❑ Stir in curry powder and salt.

❑ Add cooked rice to wok and blend well with sauce. Immediately reduce heat to low.

❑ Stir in cashew halves and butter or margarine.

   NOTE: If desired, more butter or margarine may be added to reduce spiciness.

❑ Sprinkle reserved raw onion and bread crumbs over top of rice. Mix well with rice. Turn off heat.

❑ Garnish with coriander. Reheat before serving.

Serves 8 to 10.

Black Pepper Rice
(Milagu Saathum)

2 cups extra long grain white rice
4 cups water
5 tablespoons corn oil
3 to 4 curry leaves (optional)
3 dried red chili peppers
2 teaspoons mustard seeds
3 teaspoons urad dal
2 cups yellow onion, chopped
4 teaspoons black pepper and cumin powder
2 tablespoons margarine or butter
1 teaspoon salt
2 teaspoons fresh coriander, minced (optional)

❑ Cook rice in rice cooker, or cook rice in 4 cups of water following directions for fluffy rice but omitting salt and oil if included in the directions. Cool rice about one hour, so grains do not stick together.

❑ Heat oil in a wok or in a large skillet over medium high heat. When oil is hot, but not smoking, add curry leaves and red peppers. Stir briefly. Add mustard seeds and urad dal. Cover and heat until mustard seeds burst (listen for popping sound) and urad dal is golden brown.

❑ Add chopped onion and cook for a minute.

❑ Add cooked rice and stir well with spoon into the onion mixture.

❑ Add black pepper and cumin powder to rice

❑ Add margarine or butter and salt. Mix well.

❑ Sprinkle coriander on top of rice as a garnish. Keep rice warm until serving time or reheat rice before serving.

Serves 6 to 8.

Coconut Rice

3 cups fresh shredded coconut (about 1 large coconut)
¼ cup corn oil
½ teaspoon asafoetida powder
2 dried red chili peppers
6 curry leaves (optional)
1½ teaspoons black mustard seeds
1½ teaspoons urad dal
¼ cup cashew halves (raw or roasted)
2 cups long grain rice cooked in 4 cups of water and cooled
2 teaspoons butter
1 teaspoon salt (more if desired)
¼ cup chopped coriander

❏ Peel brown skin from coconut and grind meat finely in a blender.

❏ Roast the shredded coconut by itself in a wok, stirring constantly, until golden (approximately 3 minutes). Remove coconut from wok and set aside.

❏ Heat oil in wok. When oil is hot, but not smoking, add asafoetida, dried red chili peppers, and curry leaves. Add mustard seeds and urad dal. Fry until mustard seeds pop and urad dal turns golden.

❏ Add cashews to the wok and fry for 2 to 3 minutes.

❏ Add cooked rice to the wok and mix well with nuts and spices.

❏ Stir in the roasted coconut and mix rice well with coconut and other ingredients.

❏ Add butter, salt and coriander. Mix well.

This recipe is particularly delicious served with cauliflower curry.

Carrot Rice: Shredded carrots may be used in place of shredded coconut in the above recipe.

Apple Rice: Shredded Granny Smith (firm tart green apples) may be used in place of shredded coconut in the above recipe.

Serves 6 to 8.

Lemon Rice

2 cups extra long grain rice
$\frac{1}{2}$ cup dry yellow split peas
$\frac{1}{2}$ cup lemon juice
2 teaspoons salt
$1\frac{1}{2}$ teaspoons turmeric powder
3 tablespoons corn oil
1 dried red chili pepper
$\frac{1}{2}$ teaspoon asafoetida powder
$1\frac{1}{2}$ teaspoons black mustard seeds
2 teaspoons urad dal
$1\frac{1}{2}$ teaspoons poodhi powder (identical to chutney powder,
   available   in Indian grocery stores)
2 tablespoons butter or margarine
1 green chili pepper, minced (optional)
2 tablespoons fresh coriander leaves or green onions (for
   garnish)
2 tablespoons cashew nut halves or peanuts (for garnish)

❏ Cook rice in 4 cups of water, following directions for fluffy rice but omitting salt and oil if included in directions. Cool rice about one hour, so grains do not stick together. If time is limited, a little of the lemon juice mixture can be stirred into the cooling rice to help separate the grains.

❏ Soak split peas in warm water for $\frac{1}{2}$ to $\frac{3}{4}$ of an hour; drain water. Set aside.

❏ Combine lemon juice, salt and turmeric powder; set aside. If fresh lemon juice is used, use only $\frac{1}{4}$ cup of pure juice and dilute with $\frac{1}{4}$ cup of water.

❏ Heat oil in a large skillet or wok over medium heat. When oil is hot, but not smoking, stir in red chili pepper, asafoetida, mustard seeds and urad dal. Cover and heat until mustard seeds burst (listen for popping sound) and urad dal is golden.

❏ Immediately stir in soaked split peas. Cook, uncovered, for 2 to 5 minutes, reducing heat if mixture starts to bubble. (The longer split peas are fried, the crunchier they will be.)

❑ Immediately stir in lemon juice mixture and poodhi powder. Simmer 2 to 4 minutes, reducing heat if mixture starts to boil.

❑ Reduce heat to low. Add cooked rice and stir well with mixture. Blend in butter or margarine. Add green chili.

❑ Taste and add additional seasonings, if desired. Serve garnished with coriander leaves and cashew halves or peanuts.

Serves 6 to 8.

Sweet Pongal Rice

2 cups long grain rice
5 cups 2% milk (divided)
3 cups dark brown sugar
¼ teaspoon saffron
½ teaspoon powdered cardamom
2 tablespoons raisins (more if desired)
¼ cup raw cashews or unsalted roasted cashews

❑ Cook 2 cups of rice with 2 cups milk and 4 cups   water in a slow cooker or any non-stick saucepan.

❑ To the cooked rice add remaining milk and 3 cups of dark brown sugar together with the saffron, powdered cardamom, and raisins. Stir all ingredients and leave in slow cooker for 3 to 4 hours. If cooking on the stove, cook mixture covered, over low heat for 1 hour, stirring frequently.

❑ Fry raw cashews to a golden brown in butter and add to rice mixture when it is cooked. You may also use unsalted roasted cashews.

Serves 6 to 8.

Tamarind Rice

2 cups extra long grain white rice
¼ cup yellow split peas
1¼ cups water (divided)
2 teaspoons tamarind paste
2 teaspoons salt
¼ cup corn oil
1 to 2 dried red chili peppers
½ teaspoon asafoetida powder
1½ teaspoons mustard seeds
1½ teaspoons urad dal
¾ teaspoon turmeric powder
1 pinch brown sugar (optional)
1 teaspoon poodhi powder (identical to chutney powder,
    available in Indian grocery stores)
¼ cup peanuts

❑ Cook 2 cups of rice with 4 cups of water in a rice cooker. When rice is done, set aside for about an hour to cool slightly.

❑ Soak yellow split peas in 1 cup of water for about one hour.

❑ Add tamarind paste and salt to ¼ cup water. Stir tamarind paste into the water to achieve a smooth consistency.

❑ Place oil in wok. When oil is hot, but not smoking, add red peppers, asafoetida, mustard seeds and urad dal. Cover and fry over medium heat until mustard seeds pop and urad dal is golden brown.

❑ Drain water from split peas and stir into hot oil in wok.

❑ Stir fry for half a minute. Add tamarind water to wok.

❑ Add turmeric powder and mix well.

❑ Add a pinch of brown sugar (optional).

❑ Add poodhi powder.

❑ When the mixture begins to boil, add rice and blend thoroughly.

❑ Add peanuts and stir into rice.

Serves 6 to 8.

Tomato Rice

¼ cup fresh coconut, cut into small pieces
4 green chili peppers (more if desired)
5 garlic cloves
4 small slices of ginger
2 cups basmati rice
4 tablespoons ghee or butter (divided)
3 to 4 small pieces cinnamon stick
1 bay leaf, crushed
1 medium onion, chopped
2 small tomatoes, chopped
½ cup chopped coriander (divided)
1 tablespoon lemon juice
1 cup cashews

❑ Grind coconut, chilies, garlic and ginger in a blender with a very little warm water (only enough to facilitate the grinding process).

❑ Wash rice thoroughly and drain.

❑ Pour 2 tablespoons ghee in a large saucepan and melt over medium heat. Add pieces of cinnamon stick and bay leaf to melted ghee.

❑ Add rice to saucepan and roast until golden brown. Transfer rice to a bowl and set aside.

❑ Add two tablespoons of ghee or butter in a saucepan.

❑ Add onion, tomato and ¼ cup of coriander to ghee or butter and cook until tender.

❑ Add the contents from the blender and one tablespoon of fresh lemon juice. Simmer for few minutes.

❑ Add 2 cups of water and continue to simmer.

❑ When the mixture is ready to boil, add rice. Cover and cook over low heat until rice is cooked (approximately 10 minutes).

❑ As soon as rice is cooked, turn off heat. Gently stir well and add cashews and remaining ¼ cup of chopped coriander.

❑ You may add more butter and raw onions chopped lengthwise to rice. *Serves 6 to 8.*

Vegetable Pulaoo Rice

2 cups basmati rice
5 teaspoons melted butter or ghee (divided)
1 bay leaf, crumbled
2 to 3 small pieces of cinnamon stick
½ teaspoon cumin seeds
1 teaspoon turmeric powder (divided)
4 cups hot water
2 teaspoons biryani paste (available in Indian grocery
    stores)
1 pinch saffron
¼ teaspoon cardamom powder
2 whole cloves
2 Idaho potatoes, washed and peeled
1 large carrot, peeled
1 package (10 ounces) frozen large lima beans
2 teaspoons salt (divided)
½ onion, chopped lengthwise
½ cup toasted cashews
¼ cup shredded beets
1 green chili pepper, chopped
¼ cup chopped fresh coriander

❏ Rinse rice thoroughly in cold water. Drain rice and set aside.

❏ Heat 3 teaspoons butter over medium heat in a saucepan. When butter is hot, but not smoking, add bay leaf, cinnamon and cumin seeds.

❏ Immediately add rice and fry over medium heat for 1 to   2 minutes to roast the rice. Stir frequently.

❏ Add half of the turmeric powder and mix well.

❏ Pour 4 cups of hot water over rice in saucepan. Stir well and add biryani paste, saffron, cardamom powder and cloves. Stir well.

❏ When mixture begins to boil, reduce heat to low and cover saucepan. Cook until the water evaporates and the rice is fluffy (about 5 minutes). Remove saucepan from stove and set aside, covered.

❏ Peel and chop potatoes coarsely.

❏ Peel and chop carrots.

- ❑ Add potatoes, carrots and lima beans to another saucepan with enough water to cover the vegetables.
- ❑ Add remaining turmeric and half the salt to saucepan and cook vegetables uncovered over medium heat until tender. Set aside.
- ❑ Place 2 teaspoons ghee or melted butter in a wok.
- ❑ Add cooked rice to a wok and stir briefly to separate rice grains. Add the drained vegetables to rice and mix gently.
- ❑ Add the chopped onion (½ onion) and ½ cup of cashew nuts.
- ❑ Add the shredded beets to the rice.
- ❑ Chop 1 green chili and ¼ cup coriander and stir into rice mixture.
- ❑ Add remaining salt and stir rice gently.

Serve vegetable pulaoo rice with onion and cucumber salad and chicken or potato kurma.

Serves 6 to 8.

Yogurt Rice

1 cup long grain white rice
2 cups buttermilk (approximate)
16 ounces nonfat plain yogurt (approximate)
1½ teaspoons salt
½ green chili pepper, chopped
2 tablespoons corn oil
1 teaspoon mustard seed
1 teaspoon urad dal
1 teaspoon cumin seeds
1 dried red chili pepper, broken in half
¼ cup fresh coriander, chopped

❏ Cook rice in 4 cups of water.

❏ When rice is done, add buttermilk and yogurt and mix well. You might use a masher to soften the rice and to achieve a creamy consistency. Be certain to mix very well. More buttermilk and yogurt may be added, if desired.

❏ Add salt and green chilies.

Yogurt rice may be eaten plain or dressed as follows:

❏ Pour oil into a small skillet. When oil is hot, but not smoking, add mustard seeds, urad dal, cumin and red pepper. When mustard seeds pop and urad dal is golden brown, pour mixture over yogurt rice. Mix well.

❏ Add chopped coriander.

❏ Leave rice at room temperature until you are ready to serve it.

Serves 2 to 4

Sambhar

Bangalore Sambhar

Bellpepper and Radish Sambhar
(Versions 1 and 2)

Black-eyed Peas Sambhar

Brussels Sprouts Kulambu

Carrot Sambhar

Eggplant and Potato Sambhar

Garlic Kulambu

Mixed Vegetable Sambhar

Moore Kulambu

Okra Sambhar

Pearl Onion and Tomato Sambhar

Sambhar for Idli

Zucchini Sambhar

Bangalore Sambhar
(Vegetables and Spices Cooked
in a Base of Creamy Dals)

Note: For all sambhar recipes which follow, Masoor dal may be substituted for toor dal, in the amount indicated in the recipe, if cooking time is limited. (For instructions for cooking Masoor dal, see Some General Tips for Cooking South Indian Dishes, (p. 23.)

¾ cup toor dal
2 Idaho potatoes, peeled
2 to 3 cups water
1 box of fordhook lima beans
½ tomato, chopped
1 teaspoon salt (more if desired)
¼ cup coconut, fresh or powdered
5 red chili peppers (divided)
3 garlic cloves
1 teaspoon cumin
¼ cup chopped fresh coriander
1 tablespoon corn oil
½ teaspoon asafoetida powder
1 teaspoon black mustard seeds
1 teaspoon urad dal

❑ Cook dal in pressure cooker according to manufacturer's directions, for about 15 minutes, until it becomes creamy, or you may soak dal for 2 to 3 hours in water and cook the soaked dal in microwave oven on high heat for 30 to 45 minutes with enough water to cover dal until dal becomes creamy.

❑ Peel potatoes and cut into large cubes.

❑ When dal is cooked, place dal water in a saucepan with 2 to 3 cups of water. Add potatoes, lima beans, tomato and salt.

❑ Cook over medium heat until vegetables are tender.

❑ Place coconut powder, red chilies, garlic and cumin in blender. Add a small amount of water to facilitate the grinding. Grind until smooth.

❑ Pour contents of blender into saucepan and stir well.

❑ Add chopped coriander and continue to simmer, covered, until potatoes are tender.

❏ Heat corn oil in a small skillet over medium heat. When oil is hot, but not smoking, add asafoetida, mustard seeds and urad dal. Fry until mustard seeds pop and urad dal is golden brown. Pour fried mustard seeds and urad dal into sambhar. Stir and serve.

This sambhar may be served over rice.

Serves 4 to 6.

Bell Pepper and Radish Sambhar (Version I)

½ cup toor dal
¾ teaspoon turmeric powder (divided)
3 whole red peppers (divided)
3 cups water (divided)
1 medium onion
½ cup coarsely chopped tomatoes
¼ cup chopped coriander
1 cup sliced white radish
2 medium green bell peppers
3 tablespoons corn oil
¼ teaspoon asafoetida powder
½ teaspoon fenugreek seeds
1 teaspoon black mustard seeds
1 teaspoon urad dal
1 teaspoon tamarind paste
2 teaspoons sambhar powder
1 ½ teaspoons salt
1 cup tomato sauce

❑ Place two cups of water in pressure cooker. In a small round cake pan, which will fit in the bottom of the pressure cooker, add the toor dal, ¼ teaspoon turmeric powder, 1 red pepper and 1 cup of water. Cook about 15 minutes in pressure cooker according to manufacturer's directions, until the dal is of a creamy consistency. (OR) you may also cook soaked dal in a microwave oven on high heat for 30 to 45 minutes with enough water to cover dal until dal becomes creamy.

❑ Chop onion, tomato and coriander. Set aside. Slice white radish and cut bell peppers in large chunks. Set aside.

❑ Pour corn oil in a large saucepan and heat it. When the oil is hot, but not smoking, add asafoetida, 2 red peppers (more if desired), fenugreek seeds, mustard seeds and urad dal. Fry covered until mustard seeds pop and other ingredients are a golden brown.

❑ Add the chopped onion, tomato, coriander and radish. Add ½ teaspoon turmeric powder and cook about 3 minutes over medium heat, stirring constantly.

❑ Add the creamy toor dal mixture from the pressure cooker, plus 2 cups of water, to the ingredients in the saucepan.

❑ Add the tamarind paste, sambhar powder and salt. Cook covered over low heat for 10 minutes.

❑ Add tomato sauce and chopped bell pepper. Cover and cook over low heat for 8 to 10 minutes. Do not overcook the bell pepper.
  Note: If the finished sambhar is too spicy, you may add more tomato sauce to taste.

This sambhar is best served over plain rice.

Serves 4 to 6.

Bell Pepper and Radish Sambhar (Version II)

Use all of the ingredients listed in Version I, plus the following additional ingredients:

½ **tablespoon corn oil**
2 to 4 red chili peppers
1½ **teaspoons dried coriander seeds**
½ **teaspoon cumin**
¾ **teaspoon yellow split peas**
1 tablespoon unsweetened coconut powder

❑ Follow Version I of bell pepper and radish sambhar through addition of tamarind paste, sambhar powder and salt, and cook for 10 minutes.

❑ Pour ½ tablespoon corn oil in a cast-iron skillet and heat over medium heat. When oil is hot, but not smoking, add red chili pepper, coriander seeds, cumin, yellow split peas and roast over medium heat until golden brown. Add coconut powder and stir one minute.

❑ Put all the above roasted ingredients in a spice or coffee grinder and grind (without water) to a powdery consistency. Set aside.

❑ When adding tomato sauce and bell pepper in the 7th step of the previous recipe, add ground spices listed above to bell pepper and radish sambhar. Stir and cook over low heat until vegetables are tender. Be careful not to overcook the vegetables.

This sambhar is best served over plain rice.

Serves 4 to 6.

Black-eyed Peas Sambhar

¼ cup toor dal
½ teaspoon turmeric powder (divided)
1 red chili pepper
3 cups water (divided)
1 cup dry black-eyed peas (or) 1 package frozen black-eyed
    peas
1 onion
1 tomato
2 tablespoons corn oil
¼ teaspoon asafoetida powder
1 red chili pepper
½ teaspoon fenugreek seeds
1 teaspoon black mustard seeds
1 teaspoon urad dal
½ cup tomato sauce
1½ teaspoons sambhar powder
1½ teaspoons salt
2 cloves garlic, crushed
¼ cup chopped fresh coriander (cilantro)

❑ Place 2 cups of water in pressure cooker. In a small round cake pan, which will fit in the bottom of the pressure cooker, add the toor dal, ¼ teaspoon turmeric powder, one red chili pepper, and one cup of water. Pressure cook about 15 minutes in cooker according to manufacturer's instructions, until the dal is of a creamy consistency. (OR) you may also cook soaked dal in microwave oven on high heat for 30 to 45 minutes with enough water to cover dal until dal becomes creamy.

❑ To 3 cups of boiling water, add 1 cup of dry black-eyed peas and ¼ teaspoon turmeric powder. Cook peas uncovered until they are tender. Set aside.

❑ Chop onions and tomatoes and set aside.

❑ In a saucepan, pour 2 tablespoons corn oil. When oil is hot but not smoking, add asafoetida, red chili pepper, fenugreek, mustard seeds and urad dal. Cover and cook over medium heat until mustard seeds pop and urad dal is golden brown.

❑ Add chopped onions and tomatoes to saucepan and stir well.

❑ Add ¼ teaspoon turmeric powder and the tomato sauce.

❑ Add sambhar powder and salt. Stir well.

❑ Add dal mix from pressure cooker and 2 additional cups of water.

❑ When mixture is ready to boil, add cooked black-eyed peas and let the sambhar simmer for about 5 minutes.

❑ Add crushed garlic and coriander and allow to simmer for another 5 to 7 minutes.

Serve over plain rice or with idlis.

Serves 4 to 6.

Brussels Sprouts Kulambu

½ cup toor dal
¾ teaspoon turmeric powder (divided)
2 red chili peppers
3 cups water (divided)
10 to 12 fresh brussels sprouts, cut in half
½ onion, chopped (more if desired)
½ tomato, chopped (more if desired)
2 tablespoons corn oil
¼ teaspoon asafoetida powder
½ teaspoon fenugreek seeds
1 teaspoon mustard seeds
1 teaspoon urad dal
½ cup tomato sauce
1½ teaspoon sambhar powder
1 teaspoon salt (more if desired)
½ teaspoon tamarind paste
¼ cup fresh coriander (cilantro), chopped

❏ Place two cups of water in a pressure cooker. In a small round cake pan, which will fit in the bottom of the bottom of the pressure cooker, add the toor dal, ¼ teaspoon turmeric powder, 1 red chili pepper and 1 cup of water. Pressure cook about 15 minutes in cooker according to manufacturer's directions, until the dal is of a creamy consistency. Set pan aside. Do not drain dal. (OR) You may also cook soaked dal in microwave oven on high heat for 30 to 45 minutes with enough water to cover dal until dal becomes creamy.

❏ Prepare brussels sprouts and chop onion and tomato. Set aside.

❏ Pour 2 tablespoons of corn oil into a sauce pan. When the oil is hot, but not smoking, add asafoetida, one red chili pepper, fenugreek, mustard seeds and urad dal. Cover and fry over medium heat until the mustard seeds pop and urad dal is golden brown.

❏ Add chopped onions, tomatoes and remaining turmeric powder to hot oil, stirring constantly.

❏ Add tomato sauce, sambhar powder and salt. Stir well. You may add more water (about 1 cup) to saucepan if you prefer a thinner consistency.

❏ Add the creamy toor dal mixture to ingredients in saucepan. Add tamarind paste and mix all the ingredients thoroughly.

❏ When the mixture in saucepan begins to boil, add brussels sprouts and coriander. Cover and cook over low heat until brussels sprouts are just tender (about 10 minutes). Be careful not to overcook.

This kulambu is best served over plain rice.

Serves 4 to 6.

Carrot Sambhar

½ cup toor dal
¾ teaspoon turmeric powder (divided)
1 red chili pepper
3 cups water (divided)
1 cup chopped onion
1 small tomato, coarsely chopped
3 large carrots, peeled and sliced
2 to 3 tablespoons fresh coriander, minced
3 tablespoons corn oil
¼ teaspoon asafoetida powder
4 to 5 curry leaves (optional)
1 teaspoon black mustard seeds
1 teaspoon urad dal
¼ teaspoon fenugreek seeds
¼ teaspoon tamarind paste
½ cup tomato sauce
2 teaspoons sambhar powder
1½ teaspoons salt

❑ Place two cups of water in pressure cooker. In a small round cake pan, which will fit in the bottom of the pressure cooker, put the toor dal, ¼ teaspoon turmeric powder, 1 red chili pepper, and 1 cup of water. Pressure cook about 15 minutes in cooker according to manufacturer's instructions until the dal is of a creamy consistency. When pressure cooker has cooled sufficiently, remove cake pan. Discard red pepper. Mash dal slightly and set aside, or you may also cook soaked dal in microwave oven on high heat for 30 to 45 minutes with enough water to cover dal until dal becomes creamy.

❑ Chop onion, tomato, carrots, and coriander. Set aside.

❑ Pour corn oil in a large saucepan and heat over medium heat. When oil is hot, but not smoking, add the asafoetida, curry leaves, mustard seeds, urad dal, and fenugreek seeds. Fry, covered, until mustard seeds burst (listen for popping sound) and other ingredients are a golden brown.

❑ Add the chopped onion, tomato, and coriander. Add the remaining ½ teaspoon turmeric powder and stir fry for 1 to 2 minutes.

❏ Add the sliced carrots and stir fry for a minute. Then add tamarind paste. Mix well. Cook, covered, over medium/low heat for 5 minutes, stirring occasionally.

❏ Add the toor dal mixture from the pressure cooker, plus 2 cups of water, to the mixture in the saucepan. Add tomato sauce, sambhar powder, and salt. The sambhar mixture should have the consistency of thick soup. If a thinner consistency is desired, add small additional amounts of water. Cover and continue cooking over low heat for another 5 to 10 minutes, until the carrots are tender.

This sambhar is delicious served with rice, dosai, idli, or chappati.

Serves 4 to 6.

Eggplant and Potato Sambhar

½ eggplant
1 large potato
½ onion
1 small tomato
3 tablespoons corn oil
¼ teaspoon asafoetida powder
1 whole red chili pepper
¼ teaspoon fenugreek seeds
1 teaspoon black mustard seeds
1 teaspoon urad dal
½ teaspoon turmeric powder
1 cup tomato sauce
1 cup water
¼ teaspoon tamarind paste
1½ teaspoons sambhar powder
1½ teaspoons salt, more if desired
¼ cup chopped fresh coriander (cilantro)

❑ Cut eggplant and potato into small pieces.

❑ Chop onion and tomato.

❑ Pour corn oil into pressure cooker or saucepan. When oil is hot, but not smoking, add asafoetida, red pepper, fenugreek, mustard seeds and urad dal.

❑ Cover and fry until mustard seeds pop and urad dal is golden brown.

❑ Add eggplant, potato, onion and tomato to pressure cooker.

❑ Add turmeric powder and stir fry for a few minutes over medium heat.

❑ Add tomato sauce and one cup of water.

❑ Add tamarind paste, sambhar powder, salt and chopped coriander.

❑ Stir well. Be sure that there is enough liquid to cover the vegetables.

❑ Cover pressure cooker and pressure cook according to manufacturer's directions over medium heat for 10 minutes. Check for doneness. If the potatoes are not tender, cook the sambhar for an additional few minutes in the open pressure cooker over low heat, or cook the above ingredients in the saucepan over low heat until the potatoes are tender.

Sambhar

This sambhar can be served over plain rice or as a side dish or with chappati or french bread.

Serves 4 to 6.

Garlic Kulambu

3 tablespoons corn oil
$\frac{1}{4}$ teaspoon powdered asafoetida
5 to 6 curry leaves (optional)
$\frac{1}{2}$ teaspoon fenugreek seeds
1 teaspoon black mustard seeds
1 teaspoon urad dal
1 cup chopped onion
1 cup chopped tomato
1 cup whole garlic cloves (about 3 bulbs)
$\frac{1}{2}$ teaspoon turmeric powder
$1\frac{1}{2}$ cups tomato sauce
1 cup water
$1\frac{1}{2}$ teaspoons sambhar powder
1 teaspoon red pepper powder (optional)
1 teaspoon salt (more if desired)
$\frac{1}{2}$ cup minced fresh coriander (cilantro)
$\frac{1}{2}$ teaspoon tamarind paste

❏ Add corn oil to heavy saucepan. When oil is hot, but not smoking, add asafoetida powder and curry leaves.

❏ Immediately add fenugreek, mustard seeds and urad dal. Stir quickly and cover. Fry until mustard seeds burst (listen for popping sound) and urad dal is golden (about 30 seconds).

❏ Add chopped onion, tomato, and garlic. Stir fry for a minute. Add turmeric powder and mix well. Cook, covered, for approximately 3 minutes, until onion is tender.

❏ Add tomato sauce and water. Stir well.

❏ Add sambhar powder, red pepper powder, and salt. Mix all the ingredients thoroughly while cooking over medium heat.

❏ Add coriander and tamarind paste. Continue to cook, covered, until garlic is tender. The cooking time will vary with the size of the garlic cloves (approximately 5 to 10 minutes). Serve hot over rice or reheat before serving.

Serves 4 to 6.

Mixed Vegetable Sambhar

$\frac{1}{2}$ cup toor dal
2 $\frac{1}{2}$ tablespoons corn oil (divided)
2 to 4 red chili peppers
1$\frac{1}{2}$ teaspoons dried coriander seeds
$\frac{1}{2}$ teaspoon cumin
$\frac{3}{4}$ teaspoon yellow split peas
1 tablespoon unsweetened coconut powder
2 Idaho potatoes, washed, peeled and cut into small cubes
2 green bell peppers, cut into small pieces
1 small onion, cut into lengthwise pieces
2 small tomatoes, chopped
$\frac{1}{4}$ teaspoon asafoetida
1 red pepper
1 teaspoon mustard seeds
1 teaspoon urad dal
$\frac{1}{2}$ teaspoon turmeric powder
1 teaspoon salt
$\frac{1}{4}$ cup chopped coriander leaves

❑ Cook dal to a creamy consistency in a pressure cooker according to manufacturer's instructions. You may cook soaked dal in a microwave oven on high heat for 30 to 45 minutes with enough water to cover dal until dal becomes creamy.

❑ Pour $\frac{1}{2}$ tablespoon corn oil in a cast-iron skillet and heat over medium heat. When oil is hot, but not smoking, add red chili pepper, coriander seeds, cumin, and yellow split peas and roast over medium heat until golden brown. Add coconut powder and stir one minute.

❑ Put all the above roasted ingredients in a spice or coffee grinder and grind (without water) to a powdery consistency. Set aside. Cut potatoes, bell peppers, onions, and tomatoes. Set aside.

❑ Heat 2 tablespoons corn oil in a saucepan over medium heat. When oil is hot, but not smoking, add asafoetida powder and red pepper. Immediately add mustard seeds and urad dal.

❑ When urad dal turns golden, add onions and tomatoes. Stir-fry briefly. Add potatoes together with turmeric powder. Stir well, uncovered, over medium heat.

❑ Add creamy dal water, plus additional 2 cups of water. Also add salt. Cook potatoes covered over medium heat until tender.

❑ Add ground spices to sambhar. Stir and cook covered, over medium heat. When potatoes are partially cooked, add bell peppers and fresh coriander.

❑ Cook over low heat until vegetables are tender.

This sambhar may be served with rice, idli or dosai.

Serves 4 to 6.

Moore Kulambu

2 teaspoons corn oil (divided)
1 teaspoon asafoetida powder (divided)
1 teaspoon yellow split peas
1 teaspoon long grain rice
1 teaspoon cumin seeds
2 to 3 pieces of fresh ginger
¼ fresh coconut, cut into small chunks
4 to 6 green chili peppers (more if desired)
1 cup buttermilk
1 cup water
2 whole red chili peppers
1 teaspoon black mustard seeds
1 teaspoon urad dal
1 small onion, cut lengthwise
1 small cucumber, unpeeled and cut lengthwise
1 small tomato, chopped
1 teaspoon salt
¼ cup chopped fresh coriander (cilantro)

❑ Heat 1 teaspoon corn oil in a heavy skillet. When hot, but not smoking, add ½ teaspoon asafoetida, split peas and rice. Fry to a golden brown. Add cumin, ginger, coconut and green chilies. Stir fry for a few minutes.

❑ Transfer all the ingredients from the skillet to a blender. Add buttermilk to cover the ingredients and 1 cup of water. Grind the ingredients to create a smooth mixture.

❑ Add 1 teaspoon of corn oil to a saucepan. When   oil is hot, add ½ teaspoon asafoetida, red chili peppers, mustard seeds and urad dal.

❑ Cover and fry until mustard seeds pop and urad dal is golden brown. Also add onions and stir fry for a minute.

❑ Add buttermilk mixture to the saucepan and stir well.

❑ Add cucumbers and tomato, salt and chopped coriander. Allow the mixture to cook over low heat for 2 minutes.

Moore kulambu is delicious served over plain rice.

Serves 4 to 6.

Okra Sambhar

3 cups water (divided)
½ cup toor dal
¼ teaspoon turmeric powder
2 red chili peppers (divided)
3 tablespoons corn oil
¼ teaspoon asafoetida powder
1 teaspoon black mustard seeds
1 teaspoon urad dal
1 onion, chopped
½ tomato, chopped
½ pound okra, sliced 1 to   2" thick
1 ½ teaspoons sambhar powder
½ cup tomato sauce
1½ teaspoons salt
¼ cup fresh coriander (cilantro), chopped

❑ Pour 2 cups of water into pressure cooker. In a small round cake pan, which will fit in the bottom of the pressure cooker, add toor dal, ¼ teaspoon turmeric powder, one red pepper and one cup of water. Pressure cook about 15 minutes in cooker according to manufacturer's instructions until the dals are of a creamy consistency. (OR) you may also cook the soaked dal in a microwave oven on high heat for 30 to 45 minutes with   water to cover dal until dal becomes creamy.

❑ In a saucepan, pour 3 tablespoons of corn oil. When oil is hot but not smoking, add asafoetida, remaining red pepper, mustard seeds and urad dal. Cover and cook over medium heat until mustard seeds pop and urad dal is golden.

❑ Add chopped onions and tomatoes to saucepan and stir well.

❑ Add sliced okra to saucepan and fry for 2 to 3 minutes.

❑ Add sambhar powder, tomato sauce and salt. Stir well.

❑ Add dal mixture from pressure cooker and a cup of water.

❑ When the mixture is ready to boil, add coriander.

❑ Cook, covered, over low heat for another 3 to 5 minutes.

Serves 4 to 6.

Pearl Onion and Tomato Sambhar

3 cups water (divided)
½ cup toor dal
¾ teaspoon turmeric powder (divided)
3 red chili peppers (divided)
¼ cup diced yellow onions
¼ cup coarsely chopped tomatoes
¼ cup garlic cloves, peeled and quartered
¼ cup chopped fresh coriander (cilantro)
3 tablespoons corn oil
¼ teaspoon asafoetida powder
½ teaspoon fenugreek seeds
1 teaspoon black mustard seeds
1 teaspoon urad dal
8 ounces frozen pearl onions
1 teaspoon tamarind paste
2 teaspoons sambhar powder
1 cup tomato sauce
1 teaspoon salt

❑ Place two cups of water in a pressure cooker. In a small round cake pan which will fit in the bottom of the pressure cooker, place the toor dal, ¼ teaspoon turmeric powder, 1 red chili pepper and 1 cup of water. Pressure cook about 15 minutes in cooker according to manufacturer's directions until the dal is of a creamy consistency, or you may also cook soaked dal in a microwave oven on high heat for 30 to 45 minutes with enough water to cover dal until dal becomes creamy.

❑ Chop onion, tomato, garlic and coriander. Set aside in a large bowl.

❑ Pour corn oil in a large saucepan and heat over medium heat. When the oil is hot, but not smoking, add asafoetida, 2 red peppers (more if desired), fenugreek, mustard seeds and urad dal. Fry, covered, until mustard seeds pop and other ingredients are golden brown.

❑ Add the chopped onion, tomato, garlic and coriander. Add ½ teaspoon turmeric powder and cook about 3 minutes over medium heat, stirring constantly.

❑ Add pearl onions , tamarind paste, sambhar powder, tomato sauce and salt. Cook, covered, over low heat for 5 to 7 minutes.

❑ Add the creamy toor dal from the pressure cooker, plus 2 additional cups of water, to the mixture in the saucepan. The sambhar mixture should have the consistency of thick soup.

❑ Cover and cook over low heat for 10 to 15 minutes. If the sambhar is too spicy, you may add more tomato sauce.

This sambhar is best served over plain rice.

Serves 4 to 6.

Sambhar for Idli

½ cup toor dal
2 red chili peppers (divided)
¼ teaspoon turmeric powder
5 cups water (divided)
1 potato (unpeeled), chopped
¼ large eggplant, chopped
½ tomato, chopped
1 green chili, chopped
1 teaspoon salt
1 teaspoon sambhar powder
½ teaspoon asafoetida powder (divided)
3 to 4 curry leaves or ¼ cup chopped fresh coriander
    (cilantro), optional
2 tablespoons corn oil
1 teaspoon mustard seeds
1 teaspoon urad dal
½ teaspoon cumin seeds

❏ Place toor dal, red pepper, turmeric powder, and 3 cups of water in a medium size stainless steel mixing bowl.

❏ Chop potato into cubes and add to ingredients in bowl.

❏ Also chop eggplant into small pieces and add to other ingredients in stainless steel bowl.

❏ Chop tomato and green chili and place in bowl.

❏ Add salt, sambhar powder and ¼ teaspoon asafoetida powder.

❏ Add several curry leaves or chopped coriander, if desired.

❏ Put 2 cups of water into a pressure cooker, and then the steel bowl containing all the ingredients, so that the bowl is sitting in the water.

❏ Pressure cook above ingredients in cooker for 10 to 15 minutes. (OR) First cook dal to a creamy consistency in a microwave oven. Then transfer dal to a saucepan and add all the above ingredients. Cook the vegetables until tender.

❏ Place oil in a medium sized saucepan. When oil is hot, but not smoking, add red chili pepper, ¼ teaspoon asafoetida powder, mustard seeds, urad dal and cumin seeds. Cover and fry until mustard seeds pop and urad dal is golden brown.

❏ Pour ingredients from pressure cooker, including the water, into a saucepan.

❏ Heat for a few minutes over low heat to blend thoroughly all the ingredients.

This sambhar may be served with idli, dosai or idiyappam.

Serves 4 to 6 people.

Zucchini Sambhar

2 cups water (divided)
¼ cup toor dal
1 tablespoon corn oil
½ teaspoon asafoetida powder
1 whole red chili pepper
½ teaspoon fenugreek seeds
1 teaspoon black mustard seeds
1 teaspoon urad dal
½ medium onion, cut lengthwise
1 small tomato, chopped
8 to 10 pearl onions, peeled (optional)
¼ teaspoon turmeric powder
1 teaspoon sambhar powder
¼ teaspoon tamarind paste
1 teaspoon salt
¼ cup tomato sauce
2 medium zucchini, peeled and cubed
2 to 3 tablespoons chopped fresh coriander (cilantro)

❑ Cook toor dal with 1 cup of water to a creamy consistency in a pressure cooker according to manufacturer's instructions, or use a microwave oven. Set aside.

❑ In a saucepan, heat oil over medium heat. When oil is hot, add asafoetida, whole red pepper, fenugreek, mustard seeds and urad dal. Cook covered until mustard seeds pop and urad dal is golden brown.

❑ Add chopped onion, tomato, and pearl onions. Cook 2 to 3 minutes, until onions are tender. Then add turmeric powder, sambhar powder, tamarind paste and salt.

❑ Also add tomato sauce and one cup of water and stir mixture well.

❑ Add the creamy toor dal to the above. When mixture begins to bubble, add zucchini and cook, covered, over medium heat.

❑ When zucchini is tender, add chopped coriander and simmer for an additional few minutes.

This sambhar is delicious served over plain rice.

Serves 4 to 6.

Vegetables

Acorn Squash Masala Poriyal

Green Beans Poriyal

Bell Pepper Pachadi

Bell Pepper with Onions, Tomatoes and Ginger

Broccoli with Coconut

Broccoli Podimas

Brussels Sprouts and Chick-pea Poriyal

Butter Beans Masala

Cabbage Poriyal

Cabbage and Peas Poriyal

Cabbage Kootu

Carrot Pachadi

Cauliflower Poriyal

Chick-pea Soondal

Chick-pea and Bell Pepper Poriyal

Cucumber Pachadi

Easy Sugar Snap Peas Poriyal

Eggplant Curry

Eggplant and Potato Masala

Green Peas Poriyal

Kerala Aviyal

Lima Beans Masala

Mixed Vegetable Poriyal

Mixed Vegetable Poriyal with Dried Green Peas

Mushroom Masala

Mushroom and Italian Pepper Poriyal

Okra, Onion and Garlic Mandi

Okra Curry

Fried Okra

Onion and Tomato Salad

Pasta and Cauliflower Salad

Potato Curry for Poori

Potatoes with Tomatoes and Garlic

Roasted Poriyal

Potato Kurma

Potato Masala

Roasted Masala Potatoes

Spinach Poriyal

Spinach Kootu

Tomato Pachadi

Yogurt Salad I

Yogurt Salad II

Zucchini Kootu

Fabulous

Acorn Squash Masala Poriyal

A poriyal is a dry seasoned stir-fry vegetable dish.

1 acorn squash
2 teaspoons corn oil
½ teaspoon asafoetida powder
1 red chili pepper, broken (more, if desired)
1 teaspoon black mustard seeds
1 teaspoon urad dal
1 medium onion, cut lengthwise
½ tomato, cut in chunks
½ teaspoon turmeric powder
¼ cup tomato sauce
1 to 2 teaspoons curry powder
1 to 2 teaspoons coconut powder

❏ Cut the squash into small chunks, removing the pulp and skin.

❏ Place oil in skillet. When oil is hot, but not smoking, add asafodtida powder and red pepper.

❏ Add mustard seeds and urad dal and cover. Fry until mustard seeds pop and urad dal is golden brown.

❏ Add onions and tomatoes and stir fry for one minute.

❏ Add turmeric powder and tomato sauce.

❏ Add curry powder and stir well. When the mixture begins to bubble, add the acorn squash and a small amount of water to skillet.

❏ Cover and heat over medium heat until the squash becomes some-what soft. A small amount of water may be added periodically to facilitate the cooking process.

❏ Add coconut powder and stir well.

Serve this dish with rice or bread.

Note: The same recipe may be adapted to a kolumbu (a thick sambhar) by adding more tomato sauce, water and curry powder. Also add ¼ teaspoon of tamarind paste.

Serves 2 to 4.

Green Beans Poriyal
(Green Beans with Split Peas and Coconut)

2 cups water
½ cup yellow split peas
¾ teaspoon turmeric powder (divided)
3 tablespoons corn oil
4 to   6 curry leaves (optional)
1 teaspoon black mustard seeds
2 teaspoons urad dal
1 medium onion, chopped
1 teaspoon fresh ginger, minced (optional)
1 green chili pepper, finely chopped
1 pound green beans, diced (stems removed)
1 teaspoon salt
1½ teaspoon poodhi powder, optional (identical to chutney
    powder, available in Indian grocery stores)
¼ cup fresh or unsweetened powdered coconut

❏ Boil 2 cups of water. Add split peas and ¼ teaspoon turmeric powder.
Let split peas cook over medium heat for about 15 minutes. Drain
and set aside on counter top.

❏ Heat oil in a large cast iron skillet over medium heat with curry
leaves. When oil is hot, but not smoking, stir in mustard seeds and
urad dal. Cover and heat until mustard seeds burst (listen for popping sound) and urad dal is golden.

❏ Add chopped onion, ginger and green chilies. Stir fry for 30 seconds.

❏ Add beans and stir well. Cook over medium heat for about a minute.

❏ Add salt and remaining ½ teaspoon of turmeric powder. Mix well.

❏ Cover beans and cook over low heat without water for approximately
7 to 8 minutes. (Note: a sprinkle or two of water may, however, be
added on top of the green beans to facilitate the cooking process.)

❏ Stir in poodhi powder.

❏ When beans are tender but still crisp, add cooked split peas and
coconut. Stir well. Serve immediately or remove from heat and keep
covered until serving time. Be careful not to overcook beans.
Serves 4 to 6.

Bell Pepper Pachadi

Pachadi is a vegetable dish cooked with tamarind.

$\frac{1}{2}$ cup yellow split peas
3 cups water
$\frac{1}{2}$ teaspoon turmeric powder (divided)
2 green bell peppers, cut into small pieces
1 large onion, chopped
1 tomato, chopped
1 green chili pepper, chopped (more if desired)
3 tablespoons corn oil
$\frac{1}{4}$ teaspoon asafoetida powder
1 red chili pepper, broken
1 teaspoon mustard seeds
1 teaspoon urad dal
$\frac{1}{4}$ teaspoon cumin
$1\frac{1}{2}$ cups tomato sauce
$1\frac{1}{2}$ teaspoons salt
$\frac{1}{2}$ cup fresh coriander, chopped
$\frac{1}{4}$ teaspoon tamarind paste

❑ Boil yellow split peas uncovered in 3 cups of water with $\frac{1}{4}$ teaspoon turmeric powder for about 15 minutes, until semi-soft.

❑ Cut bell pepper into small pieces and set aside.

❑ Chop onion, tomato, and green chilies.

❑ Place oil in a saucepan. When oil is hot, but not smoking, add asafoetida powder, red pepper, mustard seeds, urad dal, and cumin. Cover and fry over medium heat until mustard seeds pop and urad dal is golden brown.

❑ Add onion, tomato, and green chilies. Fry for a few minutes.

❑ Add tomato sauce, $\frac{1}{4}$ teaspoon turmeric powder and water. Stir well.

❑ Add chopped bell pepper, salt, coriander and tamarind paste.

❑ Cover and cook over medium heat until bell pepper is tender.

This recipe is delicious served with rice, chappati and poori. You may add browned ground meat to the saucepan and simmer with the green peppers.

Serves 4 to 6.

Bell Pepper with Onions, Tomatoes and Ginger

2 tablespoons corn oil
2 to 3 small pieces of cinnamon stick
1 teaspoon black mustard seeds
1 teaspoon urad dal
1 onion, chopped lengthwise
1 tomato, chopped
½ tablespoon freshly ground or chopped ginger
½ teaspoon turmeric powder
1 teaspoon garam masala powder
1 teaspoon salt
2 bell peppers, chopped lengthwise
¼ cup plain yogurt

❑ Heat corn oil with cinnamon stick in a cast-iron skillet over medium heat. When oil is hot, but not smoking, add mustard seeds and urad dal. Fry, covered, until mustard seeds burst (listen for popping sound) and urad dal is golden brown.

❑ Add chopped onion, tomato and ginger. Stir fry for one minute over medium heat.

❑ Add turmeric powder, masala powder and salt. Mix well to obtain a thick paste-like consistency.

❑ Add chopped bell peppers and blend well with sauce. Cover and reduce heat to low. Continue cooking until bell pepper is just tender, stirring occasionally. Be careful not to overcook!

❑ Stir in ¼ cup of plain yogurt and mix well.

❑ Cook uncovered, over medium to low heat for a minute.

Option: One may also add cauliflower with bell peppers to make a delicious combination.

Serves 4 to 6.

Broccoli with Coconut

2 tablespoons corn oil
1 teaspoon black mustard seeds
1 teaspoon urad dal
¾ cup chopped yellow onion
1 bunch broccoli (including stems), coarsely chopped
1 green chili pepper, finely chopped
½ teaspoon salt
½ teaspoon poodhi powder, optional (identical to chutney
   powder, available in Indian grocery stores)
½ cup freshly ground or powdered unsweetened coconut

❑ Heat oil in a large skillet or wok over medium heat. When oil is hot but not smoking, stir in mustard seeds and urad dal. Cover and heat until mustard seeds burst (listen for popping sound) and urad dal is golden.

❑ Add chopped onion and stir for 30 seconds.

❑ Add chopped broccoli, green chili pepper, salt and poodhi powder to skillet and stir well. Cook, covered for 10 to 12 minutes. (Sprinkle water on top of the broccoli mixture to facilitate cooking.)

❑ When the broccoli is tender but still crisp, add the fresh or powdered coconut and stir well.

This recipe is an excellent accompaniment to the sambhar dishes.

Serves 2 to 4.

Broccoli Podimas

1 cup yellow split peas
1 dried red chili pepper (more if desired)
1 teaspoon fennel seeds
1 teaspoon cumin seeds
½ cup water
4 tablespoons corn oil
4 to   5 curry leaves (optional)
1 teaspoon black mustard seeds
1½ teaspoons urad dal
1 large onion, chopped
1½ teaspoons poodhi powder (identical to chutney powder,
    available in Indian grocery stores)
1½ teaspoons salt
3 ½ cups finely chopped broccoli
½ cup unsweetened powdered coconut
¼ cup fresh coriander, minced

❑ Soak split peas in enough water to cover for 1 to   2 hours. Drain peas and coarsely grind in blender with red pepper, fennel and cumin. It is best to grind the split peas in small batches. Add only enough water to facilitate the grinding process. Ground split peas should have the texture of coarse corn meal.

❑ Pour ½ cup of water in a sauce pan. Place a vegetable steamer over the water. Cover the steamer with a wet cheese cloth. Tuck the hanging cheese cloth under the steamer. Pour the split pea mixture in the steamer on top of the cheese cloth. Cover and steam for 10 minutes over medium/low heat until split peas are somewhat hard to the touch. Uncover and set aside to cool. (OR), put split pea mixture in a microwave dish and cook over high heat in microwave for 5 to 10 minutes (mixture will feel somewhat hard). Set aside and cool for 15 to 30 minutes.

❑ Heat corn oil with curry leaves in a cast-iron skillet over medium heat. When oil is hot, but not smoking, stir in mustard seeds and urad dal. Cover and fry until mustard seeds burst (listen for popping sound) and urad dal is golden.

❑ Add chopped onion to skillet and cook for 30 seconds.

❑ Add all of the split pea mixture to ingredients in skillet. Blend well. Fry over medium/low heat until the split peas become golden brown and grainy in texture (approximately 3 to 5 minutes). Be certain to stir frequently. If split peas begin to stick to bottom of skillet, add a small amount of corn oil as needed to facilitate the roasting process.

❑ Stir in poodhi powder and salt. Add finely chopped broccoli and blend well with split pea mixture. Cover and cook over low heat until broccoli becomes tender (approximately another 7 minutes). Be certain to stir frequently. Remove from heat.

❑ Sprinkle unsweetened powdered coconut over broccoli and stir well. Garnish with minced coriander. Cover to keep warm until serving.

Serves 4 to 6.

Brussels Sprouts and Chick-pea Poriyal

1 package of fresh brussels sprouts (approximately 1 pound)
1 medium onion
2 tablespoons corn oil
1 teaspoon black mustard seeds
1 teaspoon urad dal
$\frac{1}{2}$ teaspoon salt
$\frac{1}{2}$ teaspoon poodhi powder, optional (identical to chutney
  powder, available in Indian grocery stores), or 1 green
  chili pepper, chopped
1 can (15 ounces) chick-peas, rinsed and drained
$\frac{1}{2}$ cup freshly ground or powdered unsweetened coconut

❑ Coarsely chop brussels sprouts.

❑ Chop onions.

❑ Heat oil in a large skillet or wok over medium heat. When oil is hot, but not smoking, stir in mustard seeds and urad dal. Cover and fry until mustard seeds burst (listen for popping sound) and urad dal is golden.

❑ Add chopped onion and stir for 30 seconds.

❑ Add chopped brussels sprouts, salt, and poodhi powder or chopped green chili to skillet and stir well. Cook covered for 2 minutes over medium heat. Be careful not to overcook brussels sprouts.

❑ Add drained chickpeas and coconut. Mix well and cook for an additional minute.

Serves 4 to 6.

Butter Beans Masala

3 tablespoons corn oil
3 to 4 tiny pieces of cinnamon stick
1 teaspoon black mustard seeds
1½ teaspoons urad dal
1 small tomato, chopped
1 cup onion, chopped
½ teaspoon turmeric powder
½ cup tomato sauce
½ cup water
1 teaspoon homemade masala powder or red pepper
   powder
1 teaspoon salt (more if desired)
1 package (16 ounces) frozen butter beans
1 to 2 tablespoons fresh coriander, minced
2 tablespoons powdered unsweetened coconut

❑ Heat corn oil with cinnamon stick in a medium-size skillet. When oil is hot, but not smoking, add mustard seeds and urad dal. Cover and fry until mustard seeds burst (listen for popping sound) and urad dal is golden brown (about 30 seconds).

❑ Add the tomato, onion, and turmeric powder. Stir-fry for 1 to 2 minutes.

❑ Add tomato sauce, ½ cup water, masala powder, and salt. Mix well.

❑ Add frozen butter beans and blend well into ingredients in skillet. Cook, covered, over medium/low heat for 10 to 12 minutes, stirring frequently. If beans become too dry, additional tomato sauce may be added to beans as they cook.

❑ When beans are just tender, add the minced coriander and unsweetened coconut. Mix well.

Serve with chappati or poori or as an accompaniment to a rice dish.

Serves 4 to 6.

Cabbage Poriyal

2 to 3 tablespoons corn oil
4 to 6 curry leaves (optional)
1 teaspoon mustard seeds
1 teaspoon urad dal
4 cups coarsely shredded cabbage
1 onion, cut lengthwise (optional)
1 green chili pepper, chopped
$\frac{1}{2}$ teaspoon turmeric powder
1 teaspoon salt
$1\frac{1}{2}$ teaspoons poodhi powder (identical to chutney powder, available in Indian grocery stores)
$\frac{1}{2}$ cup freshly ground coconut or unsweetened coconut powder (optional)
1 egg, scrambled (optional)

❑ In a skillet, heat oil over medium heat until hot, but not smoking. Add curry leaves, mustard seeds, and urad dal. Fry, covered, until mustard seeds burst (listen for popping sound) and urad dal is golden (about 30 seconds).

❑ Add shredded cabbage, onion, green chili and turmeric powder. Mix well. Continue cooking, covered, over low heat for 1 to 2 minutes, stirring frequently.

❑ Add salt and poodhi powder. Stir well. Do not overcook cabbage.

Variation: After cabbage is cooked, stir in ground coconut or powdered unsweetened coconut to make a delicious poriyal, or whipped eggs and cook until egg is stir-fried with cabbage. Add the shredded onions with cabbage to make a delicious variation.

Serves 4 to 6.

Cabbage and Peas Poriyal

$1\frac{1}{2}$ tablespoons corn oil
1 teaspoon mustard seeds
2 teaspoon urad dal
4 to 6 curry leaves (optional)
2 cups coarsely shredded cabbage
$\frac{1}{2}$ teaspoon turmeric powder
1 cup fresh or frozen peas
1 teaspoon salt
1 teaspoon poodhi powder (identical to chutney powder,
   available in Indian grocery stores)
$\frac{1}{2}$ cup freshly ground coconut

❑ In a saucepan, heat oil over medium heat until hot, but not smoking. Add mustard seeds, urad dal, and curry leaves. Fry, covered, until mustard seeds burst (listen for popping sound) and urad dal is golden (about 30 seconds).

❑ Add shredded cabbage and turmeric powder. Mix well. Continue cooking, uncovered, over medium heat for 1 to 2 minutes, stirring frequently.

❑ Add fresh peas, salt, and poodhi powder. Stir well.

❑ Cook, covered, over medium heat. Stir occasionally.

❑ When cabbage and peas are partially cooked, stir in ground coconut. Continue cooking, covered, until cabbage and peas are just tender (approximately 6 to 8 minutes total cooking time). Do not over-cook vegetables!

Serves 2 to 4.

Cabbage Kootu

Kootu is a thick, lightly seasoned vegetable dish cooked with dal.

3 cups water (divided)
½ cup yellow split peas
¾ teaspoon turmeric powder (divided)
3 to 4 red chili peppers (divided)
1 small head of cabbage, coarsely shredded
1 small onion, finely chopped
2 fresh green chili peppers, minced
1 small Idaho potato, cut in shoestring strips (about 1¼"
    long)
3 tablespoons corn oil
2 to 3 curry leaves (optional)
1 teaspoon black mustard seeds
1 teaspoon urad dal
1 teaspoon cumin
1 teaspoon ginger, finely minced (optional)
1 teaspoon poodhi powder (identical to chutney powder,
    available   in Indian grocery stores)
1 teaspoon salt

❑ Place 2 cups of water in pressure cooker. In a small round cake pan,
which fits in bottom of pressure cooker, place split peas, ¼ teaspoon
turmeric powder, 1 red pepper, and 1 cup of water. Pressure cook
about 15 minutes according to manufacturer's instructions. Remove
cake pan from pressure cooker after cooling, but do not drain water
from split peas. Mash split peas until they are of a creamy consistency.
Pour the water from bottom of pressure cooker into split pea mixture.
(OR) you may cook soaked dal in microwave oven on high heat for
30 to 45 minutes with enough water to cover dal until dal becomes
creamy.

❑ Chop cabbage, onion, fresh chilies and potato. Set aside.

❑ Heat oil in a saucepan over medium heat. Add 2 to 3 red peppers and
curry leaves. Cover pan immediately so oil will not splatter.

❑ When oil is hot, but not smoking, add mustard seeds, urad dal, and
cumin. Cover and cook until mustard seeds burst (listen for popping
sound) and urad dal is golden.

❑ Add onion and fresh chilies. Stir briefly.

❑ Add cabbage and potato. Stir fry approximately one minute.

❑ Add remaining ½ teaspoon turmeric powder and stir.

❑ Immediately add the split pea mixture and approximately one cup of water. Liquid should just cover top of vegetables in saucepan. Add more water if necessary. Cover and cook over medium heat for 8 to 10 minutes, stirring occasionally.

❑ Add minced ginger and stir.

❑ Add poodhi powder and salt to taste.

❑ Cook a few more minutes until vegetables are tender but still crisp. Remove from heat. Serve as a side dish with rice.

Serves 4 to 6.

Carrot Pachadi
(Carrot Salad)

2 cups peeled and shredded carrots
1 green chili pepper, chopped
2 cups plain yogurt
1 teaspoon corn oil
½ teaspoon asafoetida powder
1 teaspoon black mustard seeds
1 teaspoon urad dal
½ teaspoon salt (more, if desired)

❑ Wash, peel and shred carrots and place in a bowl.

❑ Chop green chilies and add to carrots.

❑ Add plain yogurt to shredded carrots and stir well.

❑ Place corn oil in a small saucepan and heat over medium heat.

❑ When oil is hot, but not smoking, add asafoetida powder, mustard seeds and urad dal. Cover and fry until mustard seeds pop and urad dal is golden brown.

❑ Pour the cooked spices into the yogurt and mix well. Add salt and mix well.

This dish can be served with rice, poori and chapati.

Serves 2 to 4.

Cauliflower Poriyal

3 tablespoons corn oil
2 to 3 tiny pieces of cinnamon stick
¾ teaspoon black mustard seeds
1 teaspoon urad dal
1 medium onion, chopped
1 medium tomato, cut in small chunks
½ teaspoon turmeric powder
1 cup tomato sauce
1½ teaspoons homemade masala powder or red pepper
    powder
1 teaspoon salt
1 head cauliflower, cut in 1 to   1½" chunks (including
    short stems)
¼ cup fresh coriander, minced
2 tablespoons unsweetened powdered coconut

❑ Heat corn oil with cinnamon stick in a cast-iron skillet over medium
heat. When oil is hot, but not smoking, add mustard seeds and urad
dal. Fry, covered, until mustard seeds burst (listen for popping
sound) and urad dal is golden brown.

❑ Add chopped onion and tomato. Stir fry for 1 minute over medium
heat.

❑ Add turmeric powder, tomato sauce, masala powder, and salt. Mix
well to obtain a thick paste-like consistency.

❑ Add cauliflower chunks and blend carefully with sauce. Cover and
cook over medium heat for 2 minutes.

❑ After 2 minutes, taste sauce and adjust seasoning, if desired. Add
minced coriander. Cover and reduce heat to low. Continue cooking
until cauliflower is just tender, stirring occasionally. Be careful not to
overcook! Total cooking time for cauliflower is 6 to 8 minutes.

❑ When cauliflower is tender, stir in powdered unsweetened coconut.
Blend well. Note: If there is too much sauce in skillet, cook, uncovered, over low heat for an additional period of time.

This recipe is especially delicious served with coconut rice.

Delicious Variation: Grind 2 to 4 slices of ginger with 2 to 4 cloves of garlic and place in blender. Add just enough water to make a paste. Before adding cauliflower as indicated above, you may add garlic and ginger paste to the cooking mixture. Then add cauliflower. Cook over medium heat, following the above recipe.

Serves   4 to 6.

Chick-pea Soondal

1 can (15 ounces) chick-peas or garbanzo beans, drained and rinsed
1 tablespoon corn oil
1 red chili pepper
1 teaspoon black mustard seeds
1 teaspoon urad dal
½ teaspoon salt
¼ cup unsweetened coconut powder

❑ Drain chick-peas, wash and set aside.

❑ Heat oil in a medium-size skillet or wok over medium heat. When oil is hot, but not smoking, stir in red chili pepper, black mustard seeds and urad dal. Cover and fry until mustard seeds burst (listen for popping sound) and urad dal is golden.

❑ Immediately add drained chick-peas, salt and coconut powder. Mix well and stir fry for an additional minute.

Option: You my also add ½ teaspoon poodhi powder or a chopped green chili. Stir well. Or, use dried red beans, dried green peas or dried chick-peas. Soak dried beans in water over night. After soaking, cook beans in water until tender. Drain water and set the beans aside. Follow the above same recipe.

Serves 2 to 4.

Chick-pea and Bell Pepper Poriyal

1 can (15 ounces) chick-peas, drained and rinsed
1 medium onion
1 medium tomato
2 bell peppers
2 teaspoons corn oil
5 to 6 very small pieces of cinnamon stick
1 teaspoon black mustard seeds
2 teaspoons urad dal
$\frac{1}{4}$ teaspoon turmeric powder
1 cup canned tomato sauce (more if needed)
1 teaspoon curry powder
$\frac{1}{2}$ teaspoon salt (more if desired)
1 to 2 teaspoons coconut powder

❑ Drain and rinse chick-peas.

❑ Chop onion, tomato, and bell peppers and set aside.

❑ Place oil in a cast-iron skillet (or any saucepan) and heat over medium heat until oil is hot, but not smoking.

❑ Add pieces of cinnamon stick, mustard seeds, and urad dal to the oil. Cover and cook until mustard seeds pop and urad dal is golden brown.

❑ Add chopped onion and tomato and stir fry for 1 to 2 minutes over medium heat. Add turmeric powder and stir.

❑ Add tomato sauce, curry powder and salt to skillet. (More than one cup of tomato sauce may be needed to cover chick-peas). Allow the mixture to boil.

❑ Add chick-peas and chopped green peppers. Mix well.

❑ Cover skillet and cook vegetables over medium heat for about 5 minutes. Be careful not to overcook vegetables.

❑ Stir in coconut powder and serve.

This recipe is delicious as a side dish or served with rice or bread.

Serves 4 to 6.

Cucumber Pachadi

16 ounces plain yogurt
1 cucumber, peeled and shredded
1 teaspoon salt
½ green chili, chopped
1 teaspoon corn oil
½ teaspoon asafoetida powder
1 teaspoon black mustard seeds
1 teaspoon urad dal

❑ Empty the yogurt into a bowl and beat it well until it is smooth.

❑ Add shredded cucumber, salt, green chili to the yogurt. Mix well.

❑ Place corn oil in a small saucepan and heat over medium heat. When oil is hot, but not smoking, add asafoetida powder, mustard seeds and urad dal. Cover and fry until mustard seeds pop and urad dal is golden brown. Pour the spices into the yogurt and mix well.

Potato Version: Instead of using cucumbers, one may also use boiled potatoes. Peel and slice potatoes. Add to plain yogurt. Add the other ingredients as above and mix. Serve with breads, tandoori chicken or pulaoo rice.

Serves 2 to 4.

Easy Sugar Snap Peas Poriyal

½ pound sugars nap peas
1 teaspoon corn oil
½ teaspoon black mustard seeds
1 teaspoon urad dal
½ teaspoon poodhi powder (identical to chutney powder, available in Indian grocery stores), or 1 red chili pepper
½ teaspoon salt
1 medium onion, diced (more, if desired)
2 teaspoons powdered coconut

❑ Remove ends of peas and wash thoroughly.

❑ Pour corn oil in a saucepan and heat over medium heat. When oil is hot, but not smoking, add mustard seeds and urad dal. Heat, covered, until mustard seeds pop and urad dal is golden brown.

❑ Reduce heat to low and add snap peas.

❑ Add poodhi powder and salt and stir well. Cover and cook over low heat until just tender (about 5 minutes).

❑ Add onions and powdered coconut. Onion should remain crisp.

❑ Stir well and serve with rice or bread.

Serves 2 to 4.

Eggplant Masala Curry

3 tablespoons corn oil
$\frac{1}{2}$ teaspoon asafoetida powder
4 to 5 curry leaves (optional)
$\frac{1}{2}$ teaspoon black mustard seeds
1 teaspoon urad dal
1 medium onion, cut in small lengthwise pieces
1 tomato, coarsely chopped
3 cloves garlic, quartered
$\frac{1}{2}$ teaspoon turmeric powder
1 small eggplant, cut in small oblong pieces
1 cup tomato sauce (divided)
$1\frac{1}{2}$ teaspoons salt
$\frac{3}{4}$ teaspoon red pepper powder
1 to 2 teaspoons unsweetened powdered coconut
1 to 2 tablespoons fresh minced coriander

❑ Heat oil in a cast-iron skillet over medium heat. When oil is hot, but not smoking, stir in asafoetida powder, curry leaves, mustard seeds and urad dal. Cover and fry until mustard seeds burst (listen for popping sound) and urad dal is golden.

❑ Add onion, tomato, and garlic. Add turmeric powder. Stir fry for 2 to 3 minutes.

❑ Add eggplant to the ingredients in skillet. Moisten with about $\frac{1}{4}$ cup of the tomato sauce. Blend well. Sprinkle with a few drops of water and cook, covered, for approximately 5 minutes, stirring occasionally. As the eggplant continues to cook, gradually stir in the remaining $\frac{3}{4}$ cup tomato sauce as needed. Add additional small sprinkles of water to prevent the ingredients from sticking to the skillet.

❑ Add salt and red pepper powder. Stir well. Continue to cook, covered, until eggplant becomes tender and sauce is thick.

❑ Remove from heat and sprinkle with coconut powder. Stir briefly. Garnish with minced coriander and serve.

Serves 4 to 6.

Eggplant and Potato Masala

2 Idaho potatoes
4 baby eggplants, or ¼ large eggplant
2 small onions
1 small tomato
1½ tablespoons corn oil
2 to 3 small pieces of cinnamon stick
1 teaspoon cumin seeds
1½ cups tomato sauce
1½ teaspoons salt
1 teaspoon red pepper powder
1 teaspoon garam masala powder
¼ cup chopped fresh coriander

❑ Wash the potatoes. (Do not peel). Cut lengthwise into small pieces.

❑ Cut eggplant lengthwise into small pieces.

❑ Also cut onion into lengthwise pieces.

❑ Cut tomato into small pieces.

❑ Place corn oil in a heavy skillet. When oil is hot, but not smoking, stir in cinnamon stick and cumin seed. Cover and fry until seeds are golden brown.

❑ Add tomatoes and onion. Stir fry for a few minutes.

❑ Add potatoes and eggplant. Mix well and stir fry for an additional few minutes.

❑ Add tomato sauce, salt, red pepper powder and garam masala powder. Stir well. You may add ¼ cup of water if the mixture looks too thick.

❑ Cover and cook over medium low heat until vegetables are tender.

❑ Add chopped coriander and mix well.

Serves 4 to 6.

Green Peas Poriyal

1 can sweet green peas (approx. 17ounces), drained
2 teaspoons corn oil
2 to 3 curry leaves (optional)
1 teaspoon black mustard seeds
1 teaspoon urad dal
1 small onion, chopped
1 green chili pepper, chopped (or) 1 dried red chili pepper
½ teaspoon salt (more, if desired)
1 teaspoon poodhi powder (optional)
1 tablespoon powdered coconut

❑ Drain water from canned peas.

❑ In a skillet, pour 2 teaspoons of corn oil. When oil is hot, but not smoking, add curry leaves, mustard seeds and urad dal. Cook, covered, until mustard seeds pop and urad dal is golden brown.

❑ Add onion and chilies and stir fry for a minute. Add drained peas.

❑ Add salt and poodhi powder and stir gently, being careful not to mash the peas.

❑ Add the coconut powder and stir gently.

Serves 2.

Kerala Aviyal

2 Idaho potatoes, washed, peeled and cut lengthwise, approximately $1\frac{1}{2}$ x $\frac{1}{2}$"
12 green beans, cut in half (same size as potatoes)
2 carrots, peeled and cut same size as potatoes
1 bell pepper, cut lengthwise
$\frac{1}{2}$ box of fordhook (large) lima beans
$\frac{1}{2}$ teaspoon turmeric powder
$\frac{1}{2}$ teaspoon salt
$\frac{1}{3}$ cup of fresh coconut, chopped coarsely
1 teaspoon cumin
3 small slices of ginger
4 green chili peppers, more if desired
$\frac{3}{4}$ cup buttermilk (divided)

❑ Cut potatoes, green beans, carrots and bell pepper and place first three ingredients in a large saucepan. Set bell pepper aside.

❑ Add $\frac{1}{2}$ box of lima beans and enough water to cover the vegetables.

❑ Add turmeric powder and salt.

❑ Cover saucepan and cook vegetables over medium heat until tender. Be careful not to overcook the vegetables. Set aside saucepan with vegetables.

❑ Place coconut, cumin, ginger, and chilies in blender with $\frac{1}{2}$ cup buttermilk. Grind to a smooth consistency and pour over vegetables in saucepan.

❑ Stir gently and cook over low heat until ingredients are heated through.

❑ Add bell pepper and coriander to saucepan and an additional $\frac{1}{4}$ cup of buttermilk. Simmer for 2 minutes.

Option: Warm 1 tablespoon of coconut oil with a few curry leaves and pour over the vegetables.

Serves 2 to 4.

Lima Beans Masala

1 package (10 ounces) frozen Baby Lima Beans
½ teaspoon turmeric powder (divided)
1 teaspoon salt (divided)
2 teaspoons corn oil
2 to 3 very small pieces of cinnamon stick
1 teaspoon black mustard seeds
1 teaspoon urad dal
½ onion, chopped
½ tomato, chopped
1 cup tomato sauce
2 teaspoons curry powder

❏ Cook lima beans until tender (approximately 3 minutes) in a sauce-pan with enough water to cover beans, together and with ¼ teaspoon turmeric powder and ½ teaspoon salt. Set aside.

❏ Place oil in a skillet over medium heat. When oil is hot, but not smoking, add pieces of cinnamon stick, mustard seeds and urad dal. Cover and cook over medium heat until mustard seeds pop and urad dal is golden brown.

❏ Add chopped onions and tomato and stir for a few minutes. Add remaining turmeric powder.

❏ Add tomato sauce and stir well.

❏ Add remaining salt and curry powder to skillet.

❏ When mixture begins to boil, add lima beans and ¼ cup of water.

❏ Cover and cook over medium heat until lima beans are tender. If tomato sauce thickens too much before lima beans are cooked, add additional small amounts of water. Be careful not to overcook beans.

This dish is delicious served with any rice dish (especially tamarind and lemon rice) or with bread. It also may be enjoyed as a sandwich filling for pita bread.

Delicious Variation: Use black-eyed peas (1 package frozen) in place of baby lima beans.

Serves 2 to 4.

Mixed Vegetable Poriyal

1 onion, finely chopped
1 tomato, cut into chunks
3 medium Idaho potatoes, cut into 1" cubes
1 small beet, cut into chunks
8 brussels sprouts, quartered
1 cup frozen peas, thawed but uncooked
4 tablespoons corn oil
5 to 6 very small pieces of cinnamon stick
1 teaspoon mustard seeds
1 teaspoon urad dal
$\frac{1}{2}$ teaspoon turmeric powder
$\frac{3}{4}$ cup tomato sauce (divided)
2 teaspoons curry powder
1 $\frac{1}{4}$ cup water (approximate)
2 $\frac{1}{2}$ teaspoons salt (less, if desired)
1 green chili pepper, minced (optional)
$\frac{1}{8}$ cup powdered unsweetened coconut (optional)

❑ Prepare first six ingredients and set aside.

❑ In a cast-iron skillet over medium heat, heat corn oil. When oil is hot, but not smoking, add cinnamon sticks, mustard seeds and urad dal. Cover and heat until mustard seeds burst (listen for popping sound) and urad dal is golden (about 30 seconds).

❑ Add onions and tomatoes. Stir and cook briefly. Add turmeric powder and mix well.

❑ Add $\frac{1}{2}$ cup of the tomato sauce. Stir and cook for one minute.

❑ Add curry powder and mix well.

❑ Add potatoes and beets with $\frac{1}{2}$ cup of water and the remaining tomato sauce. Blend and cook over medium heat for approximately 5 minutes.

❑ When potatoes are half cooked, add brussels sprouts with another $\frac{1}{2}$ cup of water. Stir well. If there is not enough liquid in skillet to cover vegetables, add more tomato sauce or water so that the vegetables do not stick to the bottom of the skillet.

❑ When vegetables are tender, but not mushy, add thawed peas. Blend carefully. Be certain not to overcook or mash the vegetables. Add salt.

❑ Sprinkle minced chili (if desired) and powdered coconut over top of vegetables. Stir briefly and immediately remove from heat.

Serves 4 to 6.

Mixed Vegetable Poriyal (Dried Green Peas)

$\frac{1}{2}$ cup dried green peas
$\frac{3}{4}$ teaspoon turmeric powder (divided)
$1\frac{1}{2}$ teaspoons salt (divided)
2 medium sized potatoes
1 medium carrot, cut into small slices
1 medium onion, sliced
1 tomato, sliced
3 tablespoons corn oil
2 to 3 small pieces of cinnamon stick
$\frac{1}{2}$ teaspoon fennel seeds
$\frac{1}{2}$ teaspoon cumin seeds
2 $\frac{1}{2}$ teaspoons red pepper powder (cayenne)
$\frac{1}{4}$ cup tomato sauce
3 teaspoons coconut powder

❑ Soak dried green peas in water for 6 to 7 hrs.

❑ Place peas with 1 cup of water in a round pan (about 1 deep) which will fit in bottom of pressure cooker. The pan should rest in about $\frac{1}{2}$ of water in pressure cooker. Add $\frac{1}{4}$ teaspoon turmeric powder and $\frac{1}{2}$ teaspoon salt to peas.

❑ Pressure cook peas according to manufacturer's instructions over medium heat for 5 minutes until tender. (You may also cook the soaked green peas in microwave until they are tender).

❑ Wash potatoes and cut into small cubes.

❑ Wash, peel and cut carrot into small slices.

❑ Chop onion and tomato.

❑ Pour corn oil into a large skillet or a wok. When oil is hot, but not smoking, add cinnamon sticks, fennel seeds, and cumin seeds. Stir briefly.

❑ Add chopped onion and tomato. Stir fry for 1 to 2 minutes until onion is tender.

❑ Add $\frac{1}{2}$ teaspoon turmeric powder, sambhar powder, and 1 teaspoon salt.

❑ Add tomato sauce and stir.

❏ Add potatoes and carrots with ½ cup water. Cook, covered, over low heat until vegetables are tender.

❏ Add peas and mix together. Cook, covered, over medium heat for another 3 to 4 minutes.

❏ Sprinkle with coconut powder and adjust seasoning. Add more salt if desired.

Serves 4 to 6.

Mushroom Masala

$1\frac{1}{2}$ cups (8 ounces) fresh mushrooms
1 onion
1 tomato
$\frac{1}{4}$ cup coriander
1 teaspoon corn oil
1 small stick cinnamon
1 crumbled bay leaf
$\frac{1}{2}$ teaspoon cumin
$\frac{1}{4}$ teaspoon fennel
$\frac{3}{4}$ cup tomato sauce
$\frac{3}{4}$ teaspoon curry powder
$\frac{1}{2}$ teaspoon salt

❏ Wash and quarter mushrooms.

❏ Chop onion, tomatoes and coriander. Set aside.

❏ Pour corn oil in a wok or in an iron skillet. When oil is hot, but not smoking, add cinnamon, bay leaf, cumin and fennel.

❏ Immediately add the chopped onions, tomatoes and coriander.

❏ Stir fry for a few minutes, and then add tomato sauce, curry powder, and salt. When the mixture thickens, add the chopped mushrooms and stir well.

❏ Cook mushrooms, covered, on low heat for 5 minutes.

❏ Stir and serve.

Serves 2 to 4.

Mushroom and Italian Pepper Poriyal

1½ cups (8 ounces) fresh mushrooms
3 to 4 long Italian peppers
1 teaspoon corn oil
1 teaspoon mustard seeds
1 teaspoon urad dal
1 onion, chopped
1 tomato, chopped
¼ teaspoon turmeric powder
cup tomato sauce
1 teaspoon curry powder
½ teaspoon black pepper and cumin powder
½ teaspoon salt
¼ cup coriander, minced

❏ Wash and mince the mushrooms. Mince the Italian peppers. Set aside.

❏ Pour corn oil into a wok or into an iron skillet. When oil is hot, but not smoking, add mustard seeds and urad dal.

❏ When mustard seeds pop and urad dal turns golden, add chopped onions and tomatoes. Add turmeric powder and stir fry for a few minutes.

❏ Add tomato sauce, curry powder, black pepper and cumin powder, and salt. Stir fry for a few minutes.

❏ When the mixture thickens, add mushrooms and chopped Italian peppers. Stir well.

❏ Add chopped coriander. Cook covered, over medium heat.

❏ As the sauce continues to thicken, stir-fry vegetables well and remove from heat.

Serve with rice or as a sandwich filling with bread.

Serves 2 to 4.

Okra, Onion, and Garlic Mandi (Spicy)

3 teaspoons corn oil
$\frac{1}{2}$ teaspoon asafoetida powder
1 teaspoon black mustard seeds
1 teaspoon urad dal
$\frac{1}{2}$ teaspoon cumin seeds
1 cup of fresh okra, sliced into $\frac{1}{2}$" pieces
1 green chili pepper, chopped
$\frac{1}{4}$ cup onions, chopped
8 to 10 garlic cloves, halved
$\frac{1}{4}$ teaspoon turmeric powder
2 teaspoons tamarind paste
1 teaspoon salt
1 teaspoon homemade masala powder or red pepper
   powder
$\frac{1}{4}$ cup tomato sauce
$\frac{1}{4}$ cup chopped fresh coriander
3 to 4 pieces of dried mango (optional)

❑ Place corn oil in a medium saucepan. When oil is hot, but not smoking, add asafoetida, mustard seeds, urad dal, and cumin. Cover saucepan and fry until mustard seeds pop and urad dal is golden brown.

❑ Add okra, chili pepper, onions, and garlic and fry for 2 to 3 minutes over low heat, stirring frequently.

❑ Add turmeric powder and continue to stir fry.

❑ Mix tamarind paste with $\frac{1}{4}$ cup of water in a small dish. Stir well until paste dissolves into the water.

❑ Pour tamarind water over vegetables and add an additional $\frac{1}{2}$ cup of water.

❑ Add salt, masala powder, tomato sauce and coriander. Mix well. Cover saucepan and cook over medium heat until vegetables are tender.

Option: You may add dried mango to the saucepan as the vegetables are cooking to give an authentic flavor to the recipe.

Serves 2 to 4.

Okra Curry

1½ pounds fresh okra, cut in halves, or 1 package (10 ounces) frozen cut okra
1 onion, chopped lengthwise
1 tomato, chopped lengthwise
4 tablespoons corn oil
1 teaspoon asafoetida powder
½ teaspoon turmeric powder
¼ cup tomato sauce
1 teaspoon red pepper powder (more if desired)
2 teaspoons salt
4 teaspoons powdered coconut

❑ Chop okra, onion, and tomato. Set aside.

❑ Add oil to skillet. When oil is hot, but not smoking, add asafoetida, onion, and tomato. Stir fry for a minute.

❑ Add turmeric powder.

❑ Add tomato sauce, red pepper powder, and salt. Mix well.

❑ Add okra and stir for a minute or two.

❑ Cover and cook over low heat until okra is tender.

❑ Add powdered coconut and cook for an additional minute.

Serves 2 to 4.

Fried Okra

1 pound okra, cut into 1" slices
½ teaspoon turmeric powder
1 teaspoon homemade masala powder or red pepper
powder
1 teaspoon salt
4 tablespoons corn oil
½ teaspoon asafoetida powder

❑ Cut okra and coat with turmeric powder, masala powder and salt in a bowl.

❑ Place corn oil in a skillet. When oil is hot, but not smoking, add asafoetida powder and coated okra.

❑ Fry okra over medium heat until okra becomes crunchy. More oil may be added to skillet to make the okra crunchier.

Serves 2.

Onion and Tomato Salad

1 onion
1 tomato
$\frac{1}{2}$ green chili
1 cup plain low fat yogurt
$\frac{1}{4}$ teaspoon salt

❏ Cut onion lengthwise.

❏ Chop tomato.

❏ Chop $\frac{1}{2}$ green chili.

❏ Add enough yogurt to blend well with the vegetables.

❏ Add salt.

This salad may be served with pulaoo rice, chapati or with poori.

Serves 2 people.

Pasta and Cauliflower Salad

1 cup small pasta shells
2 tablespoons corn oil
1 teaspoon black mustard seeds
1 teaspoon urad dal
½ onion, chopped
1 to 2 green chili peppers, chopped
2 cups cauliflower florets
½ teaspoon salt
½ teaspoon poodhi powder (identical to chutney powder,
    available in Indian grocery stores), more if desired
¼ cup fresh coriander leaves, chopped
½ cup cashew halves (optional)

❏ Boil 3 cups of water. When water is at boiling point, add pasta. Cook pasta until tender.

❏ In a skillet or wok, heat corn oil. When oil is hot, but not smoking, add mustard seeds and urad dal. Cover and fry over medium heat until mustard seeds pop and urad dal is golden brown.

❏ Add onions and green chilies. Stir fry for a minute. Onions should remain crisp. Then add cauliflower.

❏ Add pasta shells and stir.

❏ Add salt and poodhi powder and mix well.

❏ Garnish with chopped coriander leaves and cashew halves.

Serves 4 to 6.

Potato Curry for Poori

4 medium Idaho potatoes, quartered
1½ teaspoons salt (divided)
1 teaspoon turmeric powder
2 tablespoons corn oil
1 bay leaf
¼ stick cinnamon (or) ¼ teaspoon ground cinnamon
1 teaspoon black mustard seeds
1 teaspoon urad dal
1½ medium onions, chopped (more, if desired)
1 tomato, cut in large chunks
2 green chili peppers, finely chopped
¼ cup fresh coriander leaves
1 teaspoon chopped fresh ginger
1 teaspoon turmeric powder
1 to 2 teaspoons lemon juice
1 teaspoon curry powder

❏ Cook potatoes, covered, in boiling salted water with turmeric about ½ hour or until tender. Water should just cover potatoes. Peel and mash potatoes. (Do not add milk). Set aside and keep warm. (Potatoes may also be cooked in the pressure cooker according to manufacturer's instructions.)

❏ Heat oil in skillet over medium heat. When oil is hot, but not smoking, crumble bay leaf and cinnamon stick into oil. Stir in mustard seeds and urad dal. Cover and fry until mustard seeds burst (listen for popping sound) and urad dal is golden (if ground cinnamon is substituted, add later as indicated).

❏ Immediately add chopped onion, tomato, chili, coriander, and ginger. Cook, stirring, about 1 minute. (Onions should still be crisp, not soggy).

❏ Stir in turmeric powder (add ground cinnamon if used). Add mashed potatoes, 1 teaspoon salt and lemon juice to taste. Reduce heat to low. Stir well until seasonings are thoroughly mixed with potatoes. Stir in 1½ cups of water and curry powder. Simmer 2 to 4 minutes until seasonings are well mixed with potatoes.

❏ Taste and add additional seasonings if desired.

Note: If fresh green chilies are not available, substitute an additional teaspoon of curry powder. Potato curry may be made thicker by adding less water and may be used as a sandwich filling.

Serves 4 to 6.

Potatoes with Tomatoes and Garlic Roasted Poriyal

4 raw Idaho potatoes
$\frac{1}{2}$ teaspoon turmeric powder
$1\frac{1}{2}$ teaspoons salt (approximate)
$\frac{3}{4}$ teaspoon ground red pepper powder
6 tablespoons corn oil (divided)
$\frac{1}{2}$ teaspoon asafoetida powder
4 to 5 curry leaves (optional)
1 teaspoon black mustard seeds
$1\frac{1}{2}$ teaspoons urad dal
1 tomato, chopped
3 garlic cloves, chopped

❑ Thoroughly wash raw potatoes. Peeling the skin is optional. Cut each potato into 1" slices. Cut each slice lengthwise into shoestring-shaped pieces, approximately $\frac{1}{4}$ wide.

❑ Place potato pieces in a large bowl. Sprinkle with turmeric powder, salt and red pepper. Toss potato pieces in bowl to cover evenly with spices.

❑ Pour 4 tablespoons of the corn oil into a cast-iron skillet and heat at a medium temperature. Add the asafoetida and curry leaves. When oil is hot, but not smoking, add the mustard seeds and urad dal. Stir briefly and cover. Fry until mustard seeds burst (listen for popping sound) and the urad dal is golden (approximately 30 seconds).

❑ Add the seasoned potato pieces to skillet, together with chopped tomatoes and garlic. Cook, covered, over low/medium heat. Be certain to stir the potatoes every few minutes to prevent sticking. Cover and cook until potatoes are tender, stirring frequently.

❑ Uncover skillet when potatoes are tender and continue to fry over low heat until potatoes become crisp. Stir frequently.

❑ When potatoes are crisp, remove skillet from heat. These potatoes, an excellent accompaniment to lemon rice, may be served hot or at room temperature.

Serves 4 to 6.

Potato Kurma

Kurma is a vegetable or meat dish cooked with coconut paste and spices.

4 to 5 large Idaho potatoes, peeled and cut into cubes
½ cup coconut, chopped coarsely or unsweetened
powdered coconut
5 green chili peppers (more if desired)
¼ cup raw almonds
2 teaspoons cumin seeds (divided)
1 teaspoon fennel seeds (divided)
2 thick slices of ginger
2 teaspoons corn oil
1 bay leaf
¼ cinnamon stick, crumbled
½ onion, chopped coarsely
1 small tomato, chopped
¼ teaspoon turmeric powder
¼ teaspoon salt, more if desired
1 teaspoon curry powder
½ cup coriander, chopped

❑ Prepare potatoes (peel and cut) and set aside.

❑ Grind coconut, green chilies, almonds, 1 teaspoon cumin seeds, ½ teaspoon fennel, and ginger in blender with just enough hot water to facilitate the grinding process. (Do not add too much water. This should be a smooth, thick paste.)

❑ Place corn oil in a saucepan. When corn oil is hot but not smoking, add bay leaf, cinnamon stick, 1 teaspoon cumin and ½ teaspoon fennel. Stir and fry to a golden brown.

❑ Add chopped onions and tomatoes to saucepan and stir fry for a few minutes.

❑ Immediately add potatoes to the mixture. Add turmeric powder and stir well.

❑ Add the ground spices from the blender to the potato mixture. Mix thoroughly.

❑ Add salt and curry powder.

❑ When mixture begins to boil, reduce the heat to low. Add chopped coriander. Cover and cook potatoes until tender.

Serve kurma over plain rice or use as a side dish with bread.

Meat Variation: You may substitute chicken, lamb or shrimp for the potatoes. Stir fry the meat in the corn oil with onion and garlic before adding the kurma sauce.

Mixed Vegetable Variation: You may add beets, carrots, and peas to the potatoes. Frozen or dried green peas may be used. If using dried green peas, soak peas in water for 6 to 8 hours and then cook until tender in pressure cooker according to manufacturer's instructions, or microwave. Add cooked peas to the kurma when adding the other boiled or steamed vegetables. If using frozen peas, add to the kurma mixture after the other vegetables are tender to avoid overcooking the peas.

Serves 4 to 6.

Potato Masala

4 Idaho potatoes with skins, cut in thick slices
1 teaspoon turmeric powder (divided)
2 teaspoons salt (divided)
5 tablespoons corn oil (divided)
3 to 4 curry leaves (optional)
1 dried red chili pepper
1 teaspoon black mustard seeds
1½ teaspoons urad dal
1 cup onion, chopped
1 small tomato, chopped
¼ cup fresh coriander, minced
1½ teaspoons homemade masala powder or red pepper
    powder
2 tablespoons unsweetened powdered coconut

❑ Wash potatoes well, but do not peel. Cut in thick slices. Place potato slices in a pressure cooker with enough water to cover. Add ½ teaspoon of the turmeric powder and 1 teaspoon of the salt. Pressure cook for 15 minutes according to manufacturer's instructions. If pressure cooker is unavailable, you may cook potatoes in a covered kettle over medium heat for a longer period of time (approximately 20 to 25 minutes or until potatoes become soft). Drain water from cooked potatoes. Peel potaotes and discard peels. Set potatoes aside.

❑ In a cast-iron skillet, heat 3 tablespoons of the corn oil. When oil is hot, but not smoking, add curry leaves, red chili pepper, mustard seeds and urad dal. Fry, covered, until mustard seeds burst (listen for popping sound) and urad dal is golden.

❑ Add chopped onion, tomato, and coriander. Stir fry for one minute. Add the remaining ½ teaspoon of turmeric powder, 1 teaspoon of salt and the masala powder. Stir well.

❑ Add the cooked potatoes. Mash potatoes with a spoon as you blend them with ingredients in skillet. Cover and cook over medium heat for 2 to 3 minutes, so flavors will blend nicely. Taste for seasonings and add salt, if desired.

❑ Increase heat to medium/high and add the remaining 2 tablespoons of corn oil. Fry potatoes, covered, until a thin crust forms around them. Turn potatoes several times during the browning process. A small additional amount of oil may be added to skillet during the browning process, but be careful that potatoes do not become oily.

❑ If desired, additional chopped onion and fresh coriander may be added (in any proportion) to potatoes during the browning process.

❑ When potatoes are nicely browned, add unsweetened powdered coconut. Blend well with potatoes. Serve immediately.

Potato Masala is especially delicious served with poori or chappati. It may also be served as a sidedish with plain rice.

Serves 4 to 6.

Roasted Masala Potatoes

4 Idaho potatoes, washed and peeled
$\frac{1}{4}$ teaspoon turmeric powder
$\frac{3}{4}$ teaspoon salt
1 tablespoon sambhar powder or red pepper powder (more
   if desired)
5 tablespoons corn oil
4 to 5 curry leaves
1 teaspoon asafoetida powder

❏ Wash, peel and cut the potatoes into 1" cubes.

❏ Place potatoes in a small saucepan. Add water just to cover potatoes and bring to a boil. Do not cover saucepan. After the water boils, reduce the heat.

❏ Add turmeric powder and salt to the potatoes.

❏ Parboil potatoes. Be careful not to overcook the potatoes.

❏ When potatoes are parboiled, drain potatoes and place in a small bowl.

❏ Sprinkle sambhar powder over potatoes and shake bowl to cover potatoes with sambhar powder.

❏ Add corn oil to a cast iron skillet. When oil is hot, but not smoking, add 4 to   5 curry leaves and asafoetida powder.

❏ Add potatoes to skillet. Cook over very low heat until golden brown. Turn frequently.

These potatoes are delicious served with lemon rice or any meat dish.

Serves 4 to 6.

Spinach Poriyal

½ cup dry yellow split peas
¼ teaspoon turmeric powder
2 tablespoons corn oil
1 whole red pepper
1 teaspoon black mustard seeds
1 teaspoon urad dal
1 medium onion , chopped
1 package (10 ounces) frozen chopped spinach
1 teaspoon salt (approximate)
½ cup ground fresh coconut or unsweetened powdered
   coconut

❑ Cook split peas, uncovered , in ½ cup water with ¼ teaspoon turmeric powder over medium/high heat for approximately 15 minutes. Water should just cover split peas. If water evaporates before
peas become tender, add an additional small amount of water. When
split peas are done, drain and set aside.

❑ Heat corn oil in a cast-iron skillet over medium heat. When oil is hot,
but not smoking, stir in red pepper, mustard seeds and urad dal. Fry
until mustard seeds burst (listen for popping sound) and urad dal is
golden.

❑ Add onion and stir for 1 to   2 minutes.

❑ Add frozen spinach and ½ cup water. Blend well with mixture in
skillet. Add salt. Cover and cook over medium heat until spinach is
tender, stirring occasionally.

❑ Add drained split peas to spinach mixture. Blend thoroughly. Add
more salt, if desired.

❑ Sprinkle with coconut. Stir briefly and serve.

This recipe is excellent served with rice or chappati.

Serves 2 to 4.

Spinach Kootu

¾ cup yellow split peas
¼ teaspoon turmeric powder
1 dried red chili pepper
2 tablespoons corn oil
1 teaspoon mustard seeds
1 teaspoon urad dal
1 teaspoon cumin seeds
1 medium onion, chopped
5 cloves garlic, finely chopped
1 package (10 ounces) frozen chopped spinach
2 teaspoons salt
2 green chili peppers, chopped (more, if desired)

❑ Place 2 cups of water in a pressure cooker. In a small round cake pan, which will fit in the bottom of the pressure cooker, place the yellow split peas, turmeric powder, whole red chili pepper, and 1½ cups of water. Pressure cook 15 minutes   according to manufacturer's instructions. When sufficiently cooled, remove cake pan from pressure cooker, but do not drain water from split peas. Pour any remaining water from bottom of pressure cooker over split pea mixture. Mash split peas slightly until they are of a creamy consistency, but allow some of the split peas to remain whole. Set aside. If all of the water has evaporated from split peas, add enough (approximately ½-¾ cup) to make a creamy soup. Split peas may also be cooked in a microwave.

❑ Heat oil in a saucepan over medium heat. When oil is hot, but not smoking, stir in mustard seeds, urad dal, and cumin seeds. Fry, covered, until mustard seeds burst (listen for popping sound) and urad dal is golden.

❑ Add chopped onion and garlic. Stir fry for approximately 1 minute.

❑ Add frozen spinach to saucepan. As spinach begins to thaw, mix well with vegetables in saucepan.

❑ When spinach has partially thawed, add split pea mixture. Blend well with ingredients in saucepan.

❏ Cover and cook over low heat for approximately another 5 to 7 minutes, until spinach is done and all ingredients are thoroughly blended.

❏ Add salt and chopped green chilies.

❏ Serve immediately or keep warm until serving.

Spinach Kootu is delicious served with plain rice or chappati.

Serves 4 to 6.

Tomato Pachadi

$\frac{1}{2}$ tablespoon corn oil
2 red chili peppers (whole)
$\frac{1}{4}$ teaspoon asafoetida powder
1 teaspoon black mustard seeds
1 teaspoon urad dal
1 large onion, chopped
1 tomato, chopped
2 green chili peppers, chopped
$\frac{1}{2}$ teaspoon red pepper powder
2 cups plain low fat yogurt
1 teaspoon salt
2 tablespoons chopped fresh coriander leaves

❑ Place corn oil in saucepan. When oil is hot, but not smoking, add red peppers, asafoetida, mustard seeds and urad dal. Cook, covered, until mustard seeds pop and urad dal is golden.

❑ Add chopped onions, tomato and green chilies. Stir fry for a few minutes.

❑ Add chili powder and stir.

❑ Add ingredients from saucepan to two cups of lowfat yogurt. If you prefer a thinner consistency, you may add more yogurt.

❑ Add salt and stir. Garnish with chopped coriander leaves.

Serves 2 to 4.

Yogurt Salad I

1 cucumber
2 tomatoes
½ red onion
1 green chili pepper (more if desired)
1 teaspoon cumin and black pepper powder
½ teaspoon salt
1½ cups plain yogurt
¼ cup coriander, chopped

❑ Peel and slice cucumber. Slice tomatoes and onion, cutting in half if slices are large. Dice chili very fine. Place the vegetables in a serving bowl.

❑ Add cumin and black pepper powder and salt to yogurt.

❑ Pour yogurt mixture over vegetables and stir to coat vegetables. Taste and add additional seasonings if desired.

❑ Refrigerate at least one hour. Garnish with coriander leaves before serving.

Serves 4.

Yogurt Salad II

Red onion, cut in lengthwise pieces
green chili peppers, chopped
tomato, chopped
1½ cups plain yogurt
½ teaspoon salt (more if desired)
½ teaspoon cumin and black pepper powder
¼ cup coriander, chopped

❑ Combine the above (in any proportion desired) with unflavored yogurt. Add salt and cumin and black pepper powder to taste. Chill at least one hour before serving.

❑ To serve, garnish with coriander leaves.

This variation is especially good with Chicken Biryani (p. 171).

Serves 2 to 4.

Zucchini Kootu

Kootu is a thick, lightly seasoned vegetable dish cooked with dal.

$\frac{1}{2}$ cup yellow split peas
$\frac{1}{2}$ teaspoon turmeric powder (divided)
1 tablespoon corn oil
$\frac{1}{2}$ teaspoon asafoetida powder
2 red chili peppers
$\frac{1}{2}$ teaspoon black mustard seeds
$\frac{1}{2}$ teaspoon urad dal
$\frac{1}{2}$ teaspoon cumin seeds
1 onion, chopped
1 green chili pepper, chopped
1 teaspoon salt
$\frac{1}{2}$ teaspoon red pepper powder (optional)
4 medium zucchini, peeled and cut into cubes
$\frac{1}{4}$ cup fresh coriander, chopped
$\frac{1}{4}$ cup powdered coconut

❑ Place 2 cups of water in a pressure cooker. In a small round cake pan, which will fit in the bottom of the pressure cooker, place the yellow split peas, $\frac{1}{4}$ teaspoon turmeric powder and $1\frac{1}{2}$ cups of water. Pressure cook for 15 minutes according to manufacturer's directions. When cooker is sufficiently cooled, remove cake pan from pressure cooker, but do not drain water from split peas. Pour any remaining water from bottom of pressure cooker over split pea mixture. Mash split peas slightly until they are of a creamy consistency, and set aside. (You may also cook split peas in microwave until they are of a creamy consistency.)

❑ Place corn oil in a sauce pan. When oil is hot, but not smoking, add asafoetida and red peppers.

❑ Add mustard seeds, urad dal and cumin. Cover and cook until dal turns golden brown.

❑ Add onions, chopped chilies, and $\frac{1}{4}$ teaspoon turmeric powder.

❑ Add creamy yellow split peas and salt. Stir well.

❑ Add red pepper powder, if desired.

❑ Add chopped zucchini. Cover and simmer until zucchini is tender. Add chopped coriander and coconut powder. Stir and cook for 1 to 2 minutes.

This kootu may be served over rice or as a side dish.

Serves 4 to 6.

Non-Vegetarian

Chettinad Chicken or Lamb Poriyal

Chicken Biryani Rice

Chicken Kurma

Egg Kulambu

Egg Masala

Fish Curry

Fried Fish

*Ground Beef with Split Peas
and Coconut*

Lamb or Mutton Kulambu

Roasted Garlic and Pepper Chicken

Shrimp Masala

Spicy Shrimp Pasta

Tandoori Chicken

Vindaloo Chicken

Chettinad Chicken Poriyal

1 chicken (cut up fryer parts)
2 to 3 tablespoons cooking oil
1 bay leaf
¼ stick cinnamon (or ¼ teaspoon ground cinnamon)
1 teaspoon cumin seeds
1 teaspoon fennel seeds
1 onion, peeled and chopped
4 to 6 cloves garlic, chopped
2 to 3 slices fresh ginger, chopped
1 medium tomato, chopped
1 teaspoon turmeric powder
2 tablespoons curry powder
1 teaspoon red pepper powder
1 teaspoon black pepper and cumin powder
½ cup tomato sauce
1 teaspoon salt
½ cup coriander, chopped
¼ cup water (more if desired)

❑ Remove skin from chicken. Cut chicken into 10 to 12 medium pieces, as for fried chicken.

❑ Heat oil in a regular large cast-iron or electric skillet, over medium heat. When oil is hot, but not smoking, crumble bay leaf and cinnamon stick into oil. (If ground cinnamon is used, add later as indicated.)

❑ Add cumin seeds and fennel seeds; stir and fry for half a minute.

❑ Immediately add chopped onion, garlic, ginger and tomato. Cook, stirring, about 3 minutes until onions are tender.

❑ Increase heat a little. Add chicken and stir. Sprinkle turmeric powder over chicken. Cook and stir about two minutes to coat chicken well with turmeric.

❑ Reduce heat to medium high. Add curry powder, red pepper powder, and black pepper and cumin powder (and ground cinnamon if used).

❑ Cook and stir another 2 minutes to coat chicken well with seasonings. Add tomato sauce, salt and coriander. Cook and stir another 2 minutes.

❑ Reduce heat to medium low, add ¼ cup water. Cover and cook about one half hour, stirring occasionally, until chicken is tender. Sauce should be thick. (Tomato sauce mixed with water can be added, one tablespoon at a time, if chicken begins to stick to skillet)

❑ Taste and add additional seasonings, if desired, while chicken is still cooking.

Chettinad Chicken Poriyal can be served with lemon rice, white rice or any other kind of seasoned rice.

Variation: You may use leg of lamb, cut for stew, and follow the above recipe to make Chettinad Lamb Poriyal.

Serves 4 to 6.

Chicken Biryani Rice

Biryani is a fried rice made with basmati rice; it is either vegetarian or non-vegetarian.

For Rice:

    1 stick butter (or) margarine
    2 to 3 small cinnamon sticks
    1 bay leaf, crumbled
    2 cups basmati rice, rinsed and drained
    ¼ teaspoon cardamom powder
    1 teaspoon fresh ginger, minced
    4 cups hot water
    1 tablespoon biryani paste
    2 to 3 threads saffron
    1 teaspoon salt
    ¼ cup fresh coriander, chopped

❑ Melt butter in a large saucepan. When butter is warm, add cinnamon sticks and bay leaf. Add rinsed Basmati rice. Stir fry for 2 to 3 minutes, until rice becomes slightly roasted.

❑ Add cardamom powder and ginger, then 4 cups of hot water.

❑ Immediately add biryani paste, saffron threads, salt and chopped coriander. Mix well. Cook, uncovered, over medium heat until mixture reaches the boiling point.

❑ Cook, covered, over low heat until all liquid evaporates and rice is cooked.

❑ When rice is done, set aside to cool.

For Chicken Kurma:

    ½ cup coconut, cut in small chunks
    4 small slices ginger
    2 cloves garlic
    6 green chili peppers (more if desired)
    ¼ cup chick-pea halves (optional)
    ¼ cup almonds
    1½ teaspoons cumin seeds (divided)

1 teaspoon fennel seeds (divided)
3 to 4 small pieces of cinnamon stick (divided)
4 tablespoons corn oil
½ bay leaf, crumbled
2 to 3 small cinnamon sticks
1 cup onion, cut lengthwise (divided)
4 small wedges of tomato (divided)
2 tablespoons fresh coriander, minced (divided)
¼ teaspoon turmeric powder
2 pounds cut-up chicken (or) boneless, skinless chicken
    thigh pieces cut into small pieces
3 teaspoons salt
¼ cup tomato sauce
1 teaspoon curry powder
¼ teaspoon cardamom powder
2 tablespoons butter or margarine (optional)
½ cup salted cashew pieces

❏ In an electric blender, grind together coconut chunks, ginger, garlic, green chilis, chick-pea halves, ¼ cup almonds, 1 teaspoon cumin, ½ teaspoon fennel seeds and 1 to 2 small pieces of cinnamon stick. Use enough hot water to facilitate the grinding process (Water must be hot for coconut to blend properly). Process on high, for at least 5 minutes. Mixture should have a creamy, liquid consistency. Set kurma sauce aside.

❏ Heat corn oil with bay leaf and remaining cinnamon stick in a large saucepan. When oil is hot, but not smoking, add remaining ½ teaspoons cumin and fennel seeds. Fry until seeds are golden.

❏ Immediately add ½ cup onion, few wedges of tomato, 1 tablespoon of the minced coriander, and the turmeric powder. Stir-fry for 2 minutes.

❏ Add the chicken pieces to saucepan. Stir well and cook, uncovered, for 3 to 5 minutes over medium/high heat, until chicken becomes opaque and slightly brown.

❏ Pour kurma sauce over chicken mixture in saucepan. Add salt, tomato sauce, curry powder, and cardamom powder. Mix well. Cook, covered, over medium heat, until chicken becomes tender (approximately 15 to 20 minutes), stirring occasionally.

❏ When chicken is done, transfer cooked rice to an electric wok or a large saucepan. Add cooked chicken pieces with a little kurma sauce to rice and stir well. Reserve the remaining kurma sauce to serve with biryani rice later.

❏ Add butter or margarine to rice, if desired. Blend well. Garnish with remaining 1 tablespoon minced coriander and remaining ½ cup of sliced onion. Sprinkle cashew pieces over top of rice.

Serve immediately with kurma sauce and yogurt salad.

Simple Chicken Biryani Rice:

❏ Cook Roasted Garlic and Pepper Chicken (See page 185).

❏ Cook Basmati Rice without peas (See page 72).

❏ Combine the cooked basmati rice with roasted garlic and pepper chicken in a large saucepan or electric wok. Gently but thoroughly stir.

❏ Add ½ tablespoon butter or margarine to rice, and ½ cup onion, chopped lengthwise. Blend well. Garnish with 1 tablespoon minced coriander. Sprinkle cashew pieces over top of rice.

Variation: Use cut-up lamb instead of chicken in either of above recipes.

Serves 4 to 6.

Egg Kulambu

Kulambu is a thick sauce that can be served over rice, or it can be served with chappati or plain bread.

4 eggs
3 tablespoons corn oil
2 to 3 small pieces cinnamon stick
¼ teaspoon fenugreek
¼ teaspoon cumin seeds
¼ teaspoon fennel seeds
½ teaspoon urad dal
1 medium onion, chopped (about ⅔ cup)
½ cup chopped tomato
4 cloves garlic, coarsely chopped
1 green chili pepper, chopped (optional)
¼ cup fresh coriander, finely chopped
¼ teaspoon turmeric powder
1 teaspoon curry powder
1 teaspoon tamarind paste
1 teaspoon black pepper and cumin powder
1 teaspoon salt
2 teaspoons vindaloo curry paste
1 cup tomato sauce
1 cup water

❑ Hardboil the eggs. Peel and set eggs aside.

❑ Heat the corn oil in a saucepan over medium heat. When oil is hot, but not smoking, add cinnamon stick, fenugreek, cumin, fennel seeds and urad dal. Stir gently until urad dal is golden brown.

❑ Immediately add chopped onion, tomatoes, garlic, chilies and coriander to saucepan. Stir and add turmeric powder.

❑ When onion is tender, add curry powder, tamarind paste and black pepper and cumin powder. Add salt. Add vindaloo paste, tomato sauce and water. Mix well and allow the mixture to boil for about 2 minutes.

❑ When the mixture starts to boil, reduce the heat and allow to simmer over low heat for about 3 minutes.

❑ Score boiled eggs with cross marks on each end (i.e. cut the eggs slightly on each end) and add the eggs to the simmering sauce so that the eggs will absorb the flavor of the sauce.

❑ Spoon the sauce over the eggs. Remove from heat. Cover and let the eggs marinate in the sauce for several minutes before serving.

Serves 2 to 4.

Egg Masala

This is a thicker version of Egg Kulambu, which can be used as an accompaniment to meat or vegetable dishes. Egg Masala uses less tomato sauce.

4 eggs
2 tablespoons corn oil
2 to 3 small pieces cinnamon stick
¼ teaspoon fenugreek
¼ teaspoon cumin seeds
¼ teaspoon fennel seeds
½ teaspoon urad dal
1 medium onion, chopped (about ⅔ cup)
½ cup chopped tomato
4 cloves garlic, coarsely chopped
1 green chili pepper, chopped (optional)
¼ teaspoon turmeric powder
1 teaspoon curry powder
¼ teaspoon tamarind paste
1 teaspoon black pepper and cumin powder
1 teaspoon salt
½ teaspoon vindaloo curry paste (optional)
¼ cup tomato sauce
¼ cup coriander, chopped (plus some for garnish)

❑ Hardboil the eggs. Peel and set the eggs aside.

❑ Heat the corn oil in a small cast iron skillet over medium heat. When oil is hot, but not smoking, add the cinnamon stick, fenugreek, cumin, fennel seeds and urad dal. Cover and stir until urad dal is golden brown(about 30 seconds).

❑ Immediately add the chopped onion, tomatoes, garlic, and chili pepper to skillet. Add turmeric powder and stir briefly.

❑ When onion is tender, add curry powder, tamarind paste and black pepper and cumin powder. Add salt. Add vindaloo paste and tomato sauce. Stir well to blend all the ingredients.

❑ Add chopped coriander and stir.

❑ Cut eggs in half lengthwise. Add eggs to the sauce. Spoon sauce over the eggs. Blend eggs gently into mixture. Cover and allow eggs to marinate in the sauce for a few minutes before serving. Garnish with coriander.

Serves 2 to 4.

Fish Curry

3 tablespoons corn oil
4 to 5 curry leaves (optional)
$\frac{1}{2}$ teaspoon fenugreek
$\frac{1}{2}$ teaspoon fennel seeds
$\frac{1}{2}$ teaspoon cumin seeds
$\frac{1}{2}$ teaspoon urad dal
$\frac{1}{4}$ cup fresh coriander, minced
1 cup onion, chopped
$\frac{1}{2}$ cup garlic cloves, quartered or cut into medium size
    chunks
1 green chili pepper, cut lengthwise (more, if desired)
2 medium tomatoes, chopped
$\frac{1}{2}$ teaspoon turmeric powder
1 can (15 ounces) tomato sauce
$\frac{1}{4}$ cup water (approximate)
3 teaspoons curry powder
2 teaspoons black pepper and cumin powder
2 teaspoons salt (approximate)
$\frac{1}{2}$ teaspoon tamarind paste
2 teaspoons vindaloo curry paste
$1\frac{1}{2}$ pounds Canadian white fish, cleaned and sliced into 1
    to $1\frac{1}{2}$" steaks

❑ Heat oil with curry leaves in a large saucepan over medium heat. When oil is hot, but not smoking, add fenugreek, fennel, cumin seeds and urad dal. Cover and fry until urad dal is golden (about 30 seconds).

❑ Add coriander, onion, garlic, chili pepper and tomato. Stir for about one minute.

❑ Add turmeric powder. Blend and cook for another 30 seconds.

❑ Add tomato sauce and about $\frac{1}{4}$ cup water. Stir and cook until sauce is heated through.

❑ Add curry powder, black pepper and cumin powder, salt and tamarind paste. Stir well and allow mixture to simmer uncovered until garlic is tender (about 5 minutes).

❏ Add vindaloo paste. Blend well into mixture until sauce acquires a smooth consistency. Continue simmering sauce uncovered over low heat.

❏ When mixture begins to boil, add fish steaks and spoon sauce carefully over fish. Continue cooking over low heat, covered, for about 10 minutes until fish is opaque and flaky. Sauce should be stirred several times during the cooking process and more water added, if necessary. Use the handles of thesaucepan to swirl the sauce, rather than risk breaking the fish steaks with a spoon.

❏ When fish is done, remove saucepan from heat. Serve fish curry over white rice or chappati. If fish is not served immediately, reheat only briefly before serving.

Serves 4 to 5.

Fried Fish

**1 whole white fish or any fish of your choice, cleaned and cut
into 2" steaks**
$\frac{1}{2}$ teaspoon turmeric powder
1 teaspoon salt
**2 teaspoons homemade masala powder, or 2 teaspoons
    curry powder**
corn oil for frying

❏ Sprinkle turmeric powder, salt and masala or curry powder over fish.
Rub spices well into all sides of fish steaks. Marinate in refrigerator
for 2 to 4 hours.

❏ Shortly before dinner, deep fry marinated fish steaks in corn oil until
golden brown.

Fried fish is delicious served with rice and with any bean or cabbage dish.

Serves 4 to 6

Ground Beef with Split Peas and Coconut

$1\frac{1}{2}$ cups water
1 cup dry yellow split peas
2 teaspoons turmeric powder (divided)
2 to 3 teaspoons corn oil
1 bay leaf
$\frac{1}{4}$ stick cinnamon (or $\frac{1}{4}$ teaspoon ground cinnamon)
1 teaspoon cumin seeds
1 teaspoon fennel seeds
1 cup chopped onion
2 to 3 cloves garlic, finely chopped
1 green chili pepper (more if desired)
2 pounds ground chuck
2 teaspoons curry powder
1 teaspoon red pepper powder
$\frac{3}{4}$ teaspoon salt (or more to taste)
$\frac{1}{2}$ cup shredded coconut (unsweetened powdered or fresh)

❏ In saucepan, heat water to boiling. Stir in split peas and one teaspoon of the turmeric powder. Reduce heat to low and simmer, uncovered, about 20 minutes until split peas are tender and water is absorbed. (Add additional water, if necessary, if water is absorbed before peas are tender.) Set aside.

❏ Heat oil in a large skillet over medium heat. When oil is hot, but not smoking, crumble bay leaf and cinnamon into oil. Add cumin and fennel seeds; stir and fry one half minute. (If ground cinnamon or cumin is substituted, add later as indicated.)

❏ Immediately add chopped onion, garlic and chili and the remaining one teaspoon turmeric powder. Cook, stirring, for about 2 minutes, until onions are tender. Add ground beef and fry about 5 minutes until browned, stirring and breaking up meat as it fries.

❏ Stir in curry and red pepper powder (and ground cinnamon or cumin, if used). Cover and cook 2 minutes. Stir in salt, cover and cook another 5 minutes.

❏ Stir in split peas; cover and cook another 3 minutes. Add coconut and stir well. Taste and add additional seasonings if desired.

Note: To shred fresh coconut, cut ¾ inch chunks of coconut meat from the broken shell with a sharp knife, then cut into smaller pieces; use blender for the final shredding.
Packaged unsweetened coconut can also be substituted.

Serve as a lunch dish or use as a sandwich filling with sliced breads, pocket breads, rolls or tortillas.

Variation: Ground turkey is a delicious and healthful substitute for ground beef.

Serves 8.

Lamb or Mutton Kulambu

2 to 3 pounds leg of lamb or goat meat (mutton), cut into small pieces
2 tablespoons corn oil
1 bay leaf
2 to 4 small pieces of cinnamon stick
2 to 4 curry leaves (optional)
½ teaspoon fenugreek
1 teaspoon cumin seeds
1 teaspoon fennel seeds
1 teaspoon urad dal
1 medium onion, chopped
4 to 6 cloves garlic, chopped
1 tablespoon fresh minced ginger
½ medium tomato, chopped
1 teaspoon turmeric powder
2 teaspoon curry powder
1½ teaspoon cayenne pepper
1 teaspoon black pepper and cumin powder
1 cup tomato sauce
1 teaspoon salt (more if desired)
1 cup water
¼ cup fresh coriander, chopped
For Optional Garnish:
  1 teaspoon unsweetened shredded coconut
  ½ teaspoon cumin seeds
  ½ teaspoon fennel seeds
  1 to   2 dried red chili peppers

❏ Cut lamb or mutton into small pieces as if for stew. Remove fat. Rinse the meat under cold water several times and set aside.

❏ Heat oil in a saucepan. When oil is hot but not smoking, crumble bay leaf, cinnamon stick, and curry leaves into oil.

❏ Add fenugreek, cumin, fennel seeds, and urad dal. Stir fry until urad dal turns golden.

❏ Immediately add chopped onion, garlic, ginger, and tomato. Add turmeric powder and cook until onions are tender.

❏ Increase heat to medium high. Add lamb and stir for about 5 minutes until lamb is coated with the turmeric mixture and begins to turn pink.

❏ Add curry powder, cayenne pepper, black pepper and cumin powder.

❏ Stir and mix the powders well into meat. Add tomato sauce and salt. Cook and stir another 2 minutes. Add water.

❏ When mixture begins to boil, reduce heat to low. Cover and cook about one hour, stirring frequently, until meat is tender. Additional water can be added, about ¼ cup at a time, if the sauce becomes too thick.

❏ Add coriander. Cook meat until it becomes tender and the kulambu sauce has thickened. Once the mixture starts to boil, reduce the heat to low and cook mutton slowly until it becomes tender.

For Garnish:

Grind the unsweetened shredded coconut, cumin seeds, fennel seeds and dried red chili peppers in a spice grinder and add to the kulambu mixture to give meat a more spicy flavor.

For Mutton Poriyal: Transfer the cooked mutton to a cast iron skillet, stir-fry the mixture over high heat until the sauce thickens and the meat is drier.

Serves 6 to 8.

Roasted Garlic and Pepper Chicken

3 pounds boneless, skinless chicken (thighs or breasts)
10 garlic cloves, cut in half
1 medium onion, chopped
3 tablespoons corn oil (divided)
4 to 5 small pieces of cinnamon stick
1 bay leaf, crumbled
5 dried red chili peppers (more if desired)
1 teaspoon cumin seed (whole)
$\frac{1}{2}$ teaspoon fennel seed (whole)
1 teaspoon urad dal
$\frac{1}{2}$ teaspoon turmeric powder
1 tablespoon fresh ginger, minced
$1\frac{1}{2}$ teaspoons ground black pepper and cumin powder,
   mixed
$1\frac{1}{2}$ teaspoons salt
1 teaspoon curry powder
$1\frac{1}{2}$ teaspoons homemade masala powder (optional)
$\frac{1}{4}$ cup fresh coriander, chopped
1 cup water (more, if needed)

❑ Cut chicken into medium-size pieces.

❑ Peel garlic cloves and cut in half. Chop onions. Set aside.

❑ Add 3 tablespoons corn oil to a heavy wide bottomed cast-iron skillet. When oil is hot, but not smoking, add cinnamon sticks, bay leaf and crumbled red chili peppers.

❑ Add cumin, fennel seeds and urad dal.

❑ Add garlic and onion. Fry for 2 minutes.

❑ Add chicken, turmeric powder and ginger to skillet. Cook covered over low heat until the chicken is partially cooked.

❑ Add black pepper and cumin powder mixture, salt and the curry powder and masala powder, together with coriander. Stir well to coat the chicken with spices. Add water. Sir and cook chicken on medium heat about 20 to 30 minutes.

This chicken recipe is excellent served over noodles or rice or as a sandwich filling with yogurt salad in pita bread.

Optional: When water has evaporated and chicken is cooked, add small amount of corn oil to skillet and continue cooking, uncovered, over low heat until chicken is roasted and spices are crunchy. Stir periodically.

Serves 4 to 6.

Shrimp Masala

1 tablespoon corn oil
2 to 3 small pieces cinnamon stick
1 teaspoon cumin seeds
½ teaspoon fennel seeds
1 teaspoon urad dal
1 medium onion, chopped
1 small tomato, chopped
4 to 5 cloves garlic, chopped
1 tablespoon fresh ginger, minced
1 pound fresh shrimp, peeled and washed
½ teaspoon turmeric powder
½ teaspoon curry powder
¼ cup tomato sauce
1 teaspoon red pepper powder
1 teaspoon salt
1 teaspoon black pepper and cumin powder
¼ cup chopped fresh coriander

❏ Heat oil in a wok or electric skillet. When oil is hot, but not smoking, add cinnamon stick, cumin, fennel, and urad dal. Fry until spices are golden brown.

❏ Add onion, tomato, garlic and ginger. Stir fry for a few minutes.

❏ Add shrimp, turmeric powder, and curry powder. Cook until shrimp turn pink.

❏ Add tomato sauce, red pepper powder, salt, and black pepper and cumin powder. Stir well and simmer for a few minutes.

❏ Add chopped coriander and simmer, covered, for an additional few minutes.

Serve over plain rice or as a side dish with vegetables and chappati.

Serves 2 to 4.

Spicy Shrimp Pasta

1 cup pasta shells (whole wheat, preferable)
1 tablespoon olive oil
1 teaspoon cumin seeds
1 onion, chopped
2 to 3 garlic cloves, minced (more if desired)
1 pound raw shrimp, shelled and deveined
¼ cup cajun (or spicy) bread crumbs
¼ cup tomato, chopped
¼-½ cup fresh coriander, chopped

❑ Boil pasta until just tender. Drain and set aside.

❑ Pour olive oil into a wok or large skillet. Heat over medium heat until oil is hot, but not smoking.

❑ Add cumin to oil. Brown for a few seconds. Add onion and garlic cloves and stir fry for a few minutes.

❑ Add shrimp to skillet and fry until shrimp turn pink. Be careful not to overcook shrimp.

❑ Add cooked pasta shells and bread crumbs. Stir well.

❑ Add chopped tomato and coriander to pasta. Stir fry for an additional minute and serve.

Serves 4 to 6.

Tandoori Chicken

**Cut-up skinned chicken pieces (legs and breasts), or Cornish
hen, either whole or halved
Tandoori sauce (available in Indian grocery stores)
Butter or oil for basting
1 small onion, sliced and grilled
1 lemon**

❑ Wash chicken pieces. Dry carefully.

❑ Marinate the chicken in tandoori sauce for 24 hours.

❑ Bake chicken in the oven with a little butter or oil at 350 degrees for
40 to 45 minutes.

❑ Garnish tandoori chicken with grilled onions and serve.

❑ Quarter a lemon lengthwise and place lemon pieces around the
chicken.

❑ Chicken tastes good with lemon juice squeezed on it.

*To make chicken extra tender you may add ½ cup of plain yogurt and
marinate the chicken in tandoori sauce with yogurt.*

Serves 4 to 6.

Vindaloo Chicken

3 tablespoons corn oil
2 to 3 small pieces cinnamon stick
½ teaspoon fennel seeds
½ teaspoon cumin seeds
½ teaspoon urad dal
1½ medium onions, cut lengthwise
½ tomato, chopped
4 to 5 cloves garlic, halved
½ teaspoon fresh ginger, chopped
6 chicken thighs (skinned and with fat removed) or any
    pieces of chicken
½ teaspoon turmeric powder
1 teaspoon curry powder
1½ teaspoons salt
3 teaspoons vindaloo curry paste
2 cups tomato sauce
1 teaspoon cumin and black pepper powder
½ cup chopped fresh coriander

❑ Pour corn oil into a saucepan. When oil is hot, but not smoking, add cinnamon stick. Immediately add fennel, cumin and urad dal. Fry, uncovered, until golden brown.

❑ Add chopped onion, tomato, garlic and ginger. Stir fry for one minute.

❑ Add chicken. Mix and brown chicken well with other ingredients.

❑ Add turmeric powder, curry powder and salt. Stir well.

❑ Add vindaloo curry paste and two cups of tomato sauce. Add ¼ cup of water.

❑ Add cumin and black pepper powder.

❑ Add chopped coriander. When mixture begins to boil, reduce heat and simmer until chicken is tender. (About 20 to 30 minutes).

This chicken is delicious served over rice.

Serves 4 to 6.

Desserts

Carrot Halva

Moong Dal Payasam

Pala Payasam

Ricotta Cheese Dessert

Tapioca Payasam

Beverages

Buttermilk Drink

Indian Tea

Madras Coffee

Carrot Halva

2 carrots, peeled and shredded
½ cup whole or 2% milk
1 cup sugar
¾ teaspoon powdered cardamom
¼ cup raisins

❏ Peel and shred carrots. Set aside.

❏ In a saucepan combine milk and sugar. Boil milk over medium heat.

❏ When milk is hot, add shredded carrots and cook the carrots over low heat. Stir frequently.

❏ Add powdered cardamom. Cook carrots with milk until mixture becomes a thicker consistency. Stir frequently.

❏ Add raisins. Stir frequently. Scoop in a serving dish and serve.

Serves 2 to 4.

Moong Dal Payasam

¼ cup yellow moong dal
4 cups 2% or skim milk
½ teaspoon cardamom powder
1 ¼ cups granulated sugar
½ cup cashews, fried in butter
1 teaspoon butter or ghee (melted butter)

❏ Cook moong dal to a creamy consistency for about 15 minutes in pressure cooker according to manufacturer's dicrections, or cook dal to a creamy consistency in microwave.

❏ Mix creamy dal with milk in a saucepan and cook over medium heat for 5 to 6 minutes stirring frequently.

❏ Add cardamom, sugar and cashews and cook an additional 4 to 5 minutes over medium to low heat. Add melted butter and stir frequently.

This payasam can be served hot or cold. If you prefer to serve this payasam cold, refrigerate the payasam for 2 to 3 hours before serving. Serve payasam in a cup.

Serves 2 to 4.

Pala Payasam
(Almond Payasam with Fruit Cocktail)

¾ cup almonds, skinned
4 cups 2% milk
2 cups sugar (more if desired)
1 teaspoon saffron
1 teaspoon cardamom
1 can (10 ounces) mixed fruit cocktail

❑ Grind almonds with milk.

❑ Pour ground almond with milk in a saucepan and heat the mixture over medium heat.

❑ Add sugar, saffron, cardamom to the mixture and stir frequently.

❑ After the mixture boils, set it aside and let it cool.

❑ Open the fruit cocktail can and pour contents with syrup into the mixture. Stir gently. Leave payasam in refrigerator until it is time to serve.

Serves 2 to 4.

Ricotta Cheese Dessert

1 pound regular or low fat ricotta cheese
1 teaspoon kewra (rose) essence
1 cup white sugar
¼ cup almond halves

❑ Blend ricotta cheese and kewra thoroughly in a mixing bowl.

❑ Add sugar and stir well.

❑ Spread cheese mixture on a greased shallow baking pan.

❑ Bake at 350 degrees for 20 to 30 minutes until golden brown.

❑ Garnish with almond halves. Cool for 30 to 45 minutes.

❑ Cut into slices and serve.

Serves 6 to 8.

Tapioca Payasam

1 tablespoon butter
½ cup dry tapioca
4 cups 2% or skim milk
¼ teaspoon cardamom powder
¼ teaspoon saffron
1 cup granulated sugar
½ cup cashews, fried in butter

❑ Melt butter in a saucepan. Add tapioca and fry over low heat for a minute.

❑ Add milk and cook tapioca, covered, over low heat for 5 to 7 minutes. Stir frequently.

❑ Add cardamom, saffron, sugar and cashews and cook an additional 5 minutes over low heat.

❑ Serve in a cup.

Serves 4 to 6.

Buttermilk Drink

2 cups buttermilk
4 cups water
1 teaspoon powdered cumin
¾ teaspoon salt
⅛ cup minced coriander

❑ Mix buttermilk with water.

❑ Add cumin powder and salt. Stir well with buttermilk.

❑ Add minced coriander and stir well.

❑ Refrigerate and serve.

Serve like iced tea during hot summer months.

Serves 4 to 6.

Indian Tea

¾ **cup water**
¼ **cup milk**
1 tea bag
⅛ **teaspoon cardamom**
sugar

❏ Mix water and milk. Pour the mixture into a small saucepan and bring to a boil.

❏ Immerse the teabag. Add the cardamom to milk mixture.

❏ When the mixture rises to the top (begins to boil), remove from stove.

❏ Pour the tea into a cup. Add sugar to taste. Stir and serve.

Serves 1.

Madras Coffee

½ **cup 2% milk**
½ **cup water**
1 teaspoon instant coffee (Nescafe or Folgers)
1 teaspoon sugar

❑ In a small saucepan mix milk and water. Let the mixture come to a boil.

❑ After the milk has risen to the top (come to a boil), remove from stove.

❑ In a cup mix coffee and sugar. Pour the milk over coffee and sugar.

❑ Transfer the contents from one cup to another a few times until froth develops.

❑ Pour the coffee into a cup and serve.

Serves 1.

Index

Also of interest from Hippocrene Books . . .

Best of Goan Cooking
Gilda Mendonsa

From Goa—a region in Western India once colonized by the Portuguese—comes a cuisine in which the hot, sour and spicy flavors mingle in delicate perfection, a reflection of the combination of Arabian, Portuguese and Indian cultures that have inhabited the region.

This book is a rare and authentic collection of over 130 of the finest Goan recipes and 12 pages of full color illustrations. Starting with exotic cocktails and appetizers to set the mood, the book moves on to savory fish, poultry and meats. Some unusual vegetarian preparations—Feijoada, breadfruit curry, sprouted lentil curry—make interesting accompaniments. Also, pickles and chutneys made with mangoes, shrimp, lemons and chilies add a touch of adventure. Delicious desserts complete the meal, while a special section highlights tea-time snacks like tarts, cakes, cookies and halwas.

106 pages   12 pages full color illustrations   7 x 9¼
0-7818-0584-8 $8.95pb   (682)

Dictionaries & Language Guides

Assamese Self-Taught
160 pages   5 x 7   0-7818-0223-7 $7.95   (100)

English-Bengali Dictionary
1354 pages   38,000 entries   5 ½ x 8 ½   0-7 818-0373-X $28.95
(166)

Bengali-English Dictionary
1074 pages   30,000 entries   5 ½ x 8 ½   0-7818-0372-1 $28.95
(177)

Learn Bengali
160 pages   5 x 7   0-7818-0224-5 $7.95pb   (190)

Hindi-English/English-Hindi Standard Dictionary
800 pages   30,000 entries   6 x 9
Paperback: 0-7818-0470-1 $27.50   (559)
Hardback: 0-7818-0387-X $37.50   (280)

Hindi-English/English-Hindi Practical Dictionary
745 pages   25,000 entries   4 ⅜ x 7   0-7818-0084-6 $19.95pb
(442)

English-Hindi Practical Dictionary
399 pages   15,000 entries   4 ⅜ x 7   0-87052-978-1 $11.95pb
(362)

Teach Yourself Hindi
207 pages   4 ¾ x 7   0-87052-831-9 $8.95   (170)

Learner's Hindi-English Dictionary
758 pages   10,000 entries   5 ½ x 8 ¾   0-7818-0187-7 $22.50
(102)

Learn Kannada
160 pages   5 x 7   0-7818-0177-X $7.95pb   (122)

Intensive Course in Kashmiri
300 pages   5 x 8   0-7818-0176-1 $18.95   (129)

Learn Malayalam
164 pages   4 ¾ x 7   0-7818-0058-7 $7.95   (229)

Teach Yourself Marathi
143 pages   4 ½ x 7   0-87052-620 $7.95pb   (236)

Nepali-English/English-Nepali Concise dictionary
286 pages   6,000 entries   4 x 6   0-87052-106-3 $8.95pb   (398)

A Shorter English-Nepali Dictionary
154 pages   2,500 entries   4 ¾ x 7   0-87052-894-7 $11.95   (277)

Learn Oriya
160 pages   5 x 7   0-7818-0182-6 $7.95   (137)

English-Punjabi Dictionary Romanized
498 pages 5 ½ x 8 ½   0-7 818-0105-2 $14.95   (144)

Concise Sanskrit-English Dictionary
366 pages   18.000 entries   5 x 7   0-7818-0203-2 $14.95pb
(605)

Intensive Course in Sindhi
282 pages   6 x 9   0-7818-0389-6 $29.95   (455)

Sinhalese-English Dictionary
276 pages   20,000 entries   5 ¾ x 8 ¾   0-7818-0219-9 $24.95
(319)

Learn Tamil
160 pages   5 x 7   0-7818-0062-5 $7.95pb   (256)

A Classified Collection of Tamil Proverbs
499 pages   3,644 entries   0-7818-0592-9 $19.95pb   (699)

Learn Telegu
160 pages   5 x 7   0-7818-0206-7 $7.95pb   (320)

English-Urdu Dictionary
764 pages   6 x 9   0-7818-0221-0 $24.95   (364)

Urdu-English Dictionary
688 pages   6 x 9   0-7818-0222-9 $24.95   (368)

All prices subject to change. **TO PURCHASE HIPPOCRENE BOOKS** contact your local bookstore, call (718) 454-2366, or write to: HIPPOCRENE BOOKS, 171 Madison Avenue, New York, NY 10016. Please enclose check or money order, adding $5.00 shipping (UPS) for the first book and $.50 for each additional book.